HARDWIRED

Praise for *Hardwired*

"Miller's book is going to provide a map for readers who are yearning to understand how we know what we know to be true regarding faith and life. There will be lots of insight for those who cherish the line by Pascal—'The heart has its reasons that reason knows not of.'"

—Dr. Jim Singleton, Jr., Gordon-Conwell Theological Seminary, Associate Professor of Pastoral Leadership and Evangelism, Gordon-Conwell Theological Seminary

"Jim Miller does an excellent job of turning our questions upside down and helping us know how much we didn't know we knew. He suggests a major shift from trying to prove things to people to helping them realize what they already know. He helps us examine our assumptions and discover what has been missing in our thinking. This is an engaging and thought-provoking book. I highly recommend it."

—Rev. Dr. Clark Cowden, Executive Presbyter, Presbytery of San Diego

"Pastor Jim Miller (or *Hardwired*) has flipped my traditional thinking of Christian apologetics upside down with sound and logical intellect, peppered with Jim's quiet humor and personal vignettes. Our hearts are indeed 'God's Positioning System'—the case for Christ has been and is made. We just need to discover it!"

—Dr. John Reynolds, Executive Vice President, Azusa Pacific University, California, and Chancellor, Azusa Pacific Online University

"James Miller's book is a very readable reinforcement of the fact that God has placed eternity in each of our hearts. It helpfully supplements various contemporary apologetical arguments by highlighting the personal, practical, and existential themes familiar to all humans—themes that can touch the heart and move it in a Godward direction."

—Paul Copan, Professor and Pledger, Family Chair of Philosophy and Ethics, Palm Beach Atlantic University, West Palm Beach, Florida

"As someone who was privileged to hear Jim Miller preach for two years, I can tell you that he has the mind of a scholar, the heart of a pastor, and the ability to synthesize those features in a way that few leaders can. In this book Jim challenges many of the intellectual assumptions of traditional apologetics, which start with what we don't know, and suggests that the most compelling and heartfelt case for the Christian faith starts with what we do know. Just like in his preaching, he takes apologetics out of the ivory tower and brings it to the streets where people live."

—Adam S. McHugh, author of *Introverts in the Church: Finding Our Place in an Extroverted Culture*

"A fascinating and highly readable argument for God. Miller avoids the complicated jargon of much contemporary apologetics and argues in conversational style reminiscent of Lewis and Chesterton that many of our deepest-held convictions about the world point unavoidably to a personal God. The book will be of great help to those struggling with doubt. I warmly recommend it."

—Thomas M. Crisp, Chair of the Department of Philosophy at Biola University and Associate Director of Biola's Center for Christian Thought

"Rather than gathering evidence that demands a verdict, James Miller plumbs the depth of the human heart, showing us that the things we take for granted provide a sure foundation for deep, abiding faith. The whole approach is surprisingly fresh and compelling. Add to that Miller's gift for just-the-right analogy and his clear, spare style, and you'll know why I'm excited to recommend this book."

—Diana Pavlac Glyer, author of *The Company They Keep: C. S. Lewis and J. R. R. Tolkien as Writers in Community*

"Jim Miller is a gifted teacher, noted scholar, and talented writer. I have visited his church and have witnessed firsthand his passion for moving the truth of the kingdom of God into the lives of his parishioners. *Hardwired: What You Didn't Know You Knew* is for all of us who live with doubt and uncertainty about the Christian faith. With wisdom, insight, and clarity Jim points the way for anyone struggling with insecurity and disbelief to firmly grasp the idea that what they already know is the perfect place to realize a belief in God. This is a book I will recommend to every young adult wrestling with core and fundamental truth. It is a book I will recommend to every mature and older adult looking for a path forward through doubt, frustration, and seasons of distress. It is a book I will recommend to anyone open to the idea that God exists and that he loves them and wants them to know him. In fact I recommend *Hardwired* to you. I am certain it will open your understanding of God and deepen your belief in God."

—Jon Wallace, President of Azusa Pacific University

"Here is a fresh and original look at religious unbelief. In *Hardwired*, James Miller surprisingly argues that we all—atheists, agnostics, and believers alike—latently believe that God exists and that we depend on God. The book is clever, well-written, and convincing. I recommend it highly."

—Stephen T. Davis, Russell K. Pitzer Professor of Philosophy, Claremont McKenna College

"In a world of debate and challenge to the Christian way of thinking, this book is a breath of fresh air in giving guidance and principles of understanding of how faith really works and pulsates in one's life. Offbeat, different, creative—it's a new way of looking at how faith is given, is nurtured, and survives."

—Dan Chun, pastor of First Presbyterian Church of Honolulu, co-founder of Hawaiian Islands Ministries

"I like *Hardwired* a lot. It's smart, confident, and quite funny. Miller drills to the core of detached claims to neutrality about God. I can't wait to give this book to friends of mine."

—Tim Stafford, author of *Miracles*

HARDWIRED

Finding the God You Already Know

JAMES W. MILLER

Abingdon Press
Nashville

HARDWIRED
Finding the God You Already Know

Library of Congress Cataloging-in-Publication Data

Miller, James W.
  Hardwired : finding the God you already know / James W. Miller.
    pages cm
  ISBN 978-1-4267-7381-5 (pbk. / trade pbk. : alk. paper) 1. Apologetics. 2. God (Christianity)—Knowableness. I. Title.
  BT1103.M55 2013
  239—dc23

                                                                                    2013013883

13 14 15 16 17 18 19 20 21 22—10 9 8 7 6 5 4 3 2 1

MANUFACTURED IN THE UNITED STATES OF AMERICA

CONTENTS

INTRODUCTION

Tears

I KNEW THERE WAS a college guy out there somewhere settling into a dorm, scoping out the weekend nightlife, and generally not thinking about the fact that his flippant comment about church had brought his mother to my doorstep. She caught me on the patio after church almost in tears. She told me her son was in his first year at college and had given up on everything she had taught him about faith. Years of Sunday school instruction had amounted to firm agnosticism. So many childhood bedtime prayers had now resulted in an adulthood of sleeping in on the weekends. She described recent conversations and arguments and e-mails, which had concluded in a closed door.

"How do I convince him that there is a God?" she asked. The things I said to her were really things I wanted to say to him.

"He already believes in God," I told her. She paused and stared at me like she was trying to recognize someone she hadn't seen in years. Then she proceeded to tell me the entire story over again, as though I hadn't heard what she had said.

As she talked, she sounded like a mom who lived a long time ago, who, likewise, had gone to her local cleric in tears. Her name was Monica. Her son's name was Augustine.

Though she had brought him up in the faith, the young intellect soon came to see Christianity as a superstition of the peasantry. She also went to plead for explanations. The pastor said, "Go. It is not possible that a son of such tears would perish."[1] Her pastor was a wiser man than I.

I suspect that his words relieved a grieving mother who wanted to know she had done everything she could. I meant only to assure this mother that nothing needed to be done.

Again when she finished, I repeated, "He already believes in God."

Baffled, she stammered, "What do you mean?"

The book that follows is the answer to that question.

Current Christian apologetics has wrongly assumed the position of defense attorney protecting a loose and circumstantial body of evidence. A group of angry prosecutors regularly hack away at the defense. The nominally religious population rests easy, assuming the work of keeping religious and moral obligations at bay is being done for them.

The Bible says we are in exactly the opposite position. The Bible says that God's existence is so clear in creation that people are "without excuse" for not believing (Romans 1:20). Belief in God need not be defended, the Bible insists; rather it's the one who rejects the faith who has something to prove.

For those who don't believe, or who claim they don't believe, the issue isn't whether or not sufficient evidence can be presented to make a case for Christ. Rather, the doubtful person need only take a good hard look at what he already knows to realize that he already has every reason to believe.

Unlike other books that speak to reasons for faith, this one doesn't present evidence and arguments for the supposedly rational person to weigh. Instead it shows that reasonable people have already been assuming God's existence all along, and in fact can't go on living the way they do if they want to disclaim belief in God.

The defense of the Christian faith in the Western world at the end of the twentieth century has been like an astronomer who keeps looking "out there" to see what can be found. In fact, the work of helping people believe is more like that of a geologist, who has been standing on the evidence all along and simply needs to start digging.

For those who claim not to believe, I don't intend to persuade you to. I intend to show you that I don't need to.

REV. DR. JAMES W. MILLER
Los Angeles, CA
January 2013

1
WHAT YOU DIDN'T KNOW YOU KNEW

The Wrong Approach

THE PRIMARY OBSTACLE TO faith in God is not what we don't know. It's what we don't know that we know.

The effort of prominent modern defenders of the Christian faith has been to secure credentials that they don't need in order to prove to people something that they already know. These apologists have acquiesced to and are reinforcing the idea that only certain, qualified people can have meaningful conversations on crucial issues in the public arena. Their rolls now include the names of scientists, professors, and scholars who want to present an overwhelming rational and academic case for faith that proves that people should believe in God. For instance, Lee Strobel's popular *The Case for Christ* is written from the perspective of a reporter who flies across the country interviewing experts in various fields to assess whether or not there is reason to believe. The implication is that the public is awfully lucky to have researchers capable of doing the necessary legwork, because otherwise they might not be able to make an informed decision. These contemporary Christian leaders are hiding their clergy robes under lab coats and power suits. Intending to best the secular, academic opposition at their own game, they've declared a calculated frontal assault on the frontal lobe.[1]

It isn't going to work.

The whole enterprise is based on the assumption that the evidence of God must be found, investigated, and tested. The investigator must be objective, inquisitive, and educated. The result has not been a vast audience of convinced believers. The result has been an audience that is shrinking.[2]

I remember seeing the results of this method plainly one night.

As the millennium came to a close, in a bustling lecture hall filled with hundreds of fidgeting spectators, a sweaty, suit-clad panel of six debaters squared off over the rationale for intelligent design, evolution, science, religion, and the decision-making prowess of the board of education. A cone of light shone down over them from above so as to suggest that God had paused to pay attention.

They debated, argued, pleaded, cajoled, and concluded with complete confidence on either side of the line.

At the end of the debate, the moderator whimsically turned over his shoulder and called out into the densely packed crowd, "How many of you have actually changed your minds on the subject tonight?" He shielded his eyes from the overhead spotlights and peered into the throng. "Six," he reported. Given that both sides had presented competently, it may have been a net of zero conversions.[3]

The failure is based on two misunderstandings.

First, the most prominent contemporary defenders of the Christian faith have lost touch with human experience. The problem with their method is that they don't take into account the way that faith actually takes root in the human heart.[4] Most people who believe in anything, religious or otherwise, did not get there by listening to a debate, and meaningful beliefs do not often rest on academic research. That isn't to suggest that faith and reason are unrelated. There are those who think God gave reason to humanity the way a father gives a BB gun to his son, telling him, "You can play with that thing all you want. Just don't point it at me." To the contrary. In fact, the Scriptures say that God intends for people to come looking for him (Matthew 7:7-12). He isn't afraid of our reasoning. Rather, I mean only to say that modern apologists, bearing PhDs and trained in professional oratory, require the curious to acquire difficult educational credentials just to understand conversations about the existence of God. They imply that the casual observer doesn't have the mental faculties necessary to consider the question. The only hope for uncertain investigators is that they might rely upon a qualified biblical scholar, academic, or rhetorician who can assure them that the proofs of God's existence are in fact satisfactory. Unless they have time to go to seminary, they're just going to have to pray someone else will figure out the right answers for them. In fact, belief is not a graduation gift. You don't have to buy a telescope to look for what the naked eye can see.

If the first failure of modern defenders of Christianity is to require excessive credentials, the second is to assume that their listeners are a blank slate.[5] It's the idea that the person to whom Christianity is presented is either neutral and can make an objective decision for or against Christianity, or worse yet, justifiably skeptical and must be convinced. The pressure is then entirely on the presenter to be sufficiently persuasive. The listener remains safely unobligated.

In fact, the Bible starts in a radically different place, stating outright that everyone already has enough evidence to believe and in fact has no excuse for not believing. The Scriptures mean for this to be every bit as brash as it sounds, and its authors offer no apology. Scriptures claim that God's work can be seen in nature (Psalm 19:1-6), that humanity itself bears the irrevocable image of God (Genesis 1:27), that people's intuitions for God may actually be pointing them in the right direction (Acts 17:16-34), and that people are obligated to believe in God (Romans 1:20).

Far from being a blank slate, human beings come with things written on them in large letters.

The aim of this book is to empower the rest of us to discover that we already sense that God exists and in fact depend on God's existence. Without any technical expertise, the open-hearted and level-headed observer already has enough information to find God (Romans 1:20), because in fact God isn't far from any one of us (Acts 17:27). This is a new approach to considering faith that is far less a matter of exploring data and argumentation and more a matter of exposing the knowledge that we already carry around with us, albeit sometimes unknowingly.

You're about to find out how much you didn't know you knew.

Latent Knowledge

BRAINS DON'T WORK LIKE a blank marker board that someone comes along to write on. Sometimes things get "written" on the brain inadvertently, and then the brain itself moves around the letters. We're not entirely conscious of what we are learning or what our brains are doing with the knowledge. Our brains can distort knowledge. Sometimes our brains hide knowledge.

Sometimes we don't know what we know.

When a person remembers where he left his car keys or the remote, that memory was knowledge that he already possessed but that was somehow momentarily veiled. After all, it was he who left the keys on the roof of the car, and that memory was somewhere in his head. Perhaps he couldn't remember because he was trolling around in the frontal cortex of his brain looking for something that he was actually keeping in his hippocampus (which is also a strange place to leave keys). Sometimes people recover memories by retracing the chain of events leading up to the moment that is now veiled. They talk themselves chronologically through their memories: "Let's see. I parked; I got out; there were groceries in the back, so I had to get them . . ." And then in a moment as crisp as the striking of a match, they recall knowledge that they already possessed but somehow couldn't access. This is called latent knowledge. Latent knowledge exists somewhere in that person's brain, but it is as though there were a flashlight shining around in the attic whose beam of light simply hasn't yet come to rest on the object of interest.

Latent knowledge includes more than just something that has been forgotten. It can also be information that a person picks up in the course of normal, daily experiences without consciously reflecting on what is being learned. Athletes may have an intuitive sense for physics without being able to explain vectors. They have picked up latent understandings without stopping to identify them. They've learned velocity, trajectory, and kinetic energy while their minds were focused on hitting the ball and getting on base. There are now some ideas in the mind, secret even to them, that they picked up between first and second.

The pursuit of God in this day and age has wrongly taken a turn in the direction of looking for a God who is "out there," whose existence can be substantiated only through paleontology, astronomy, and cosmology.

Perhaps God is just in the attic.

Perhaps we have unknowingly picked up a latent knowledge of God in the normal course of our experiences and simply never stopped to notice it.

God is nearby, and closer than many people suspect. What if all of humanity unilaterally possesses latent knowledge, which, if exposed, would lead to confident belief in God? This is, as we will see, what the Bible promises and what intuition demands.

However, discovering what we already know about God requires a second kind of knowledge.

Deductive Knowledge

THERE IS ANOTHER KIND of knowledge that is similar to latent knowledge, because it's made up of ideas that a person already possesses. It's a knowledge we don't have to go find. It requires no encyclopedia or search engine. We just have to realize we've already found it.

However, unlike the car keys, it's not necessarily a something that a person has seen before and needs to remember. Instead, it's a kind of idea that one discovers by assembling other ideas we already have. It's a type of knowledge we attain by inference and deduction. It's a kind of secondary knowledge that exists in pieces yet to be assembled. Someone who has a 1 and a 1 in his head also has a 2 waiting to appear.

For instance, finding a favorite author within the pages of his or her pseudonymous novel isn't difficult. The story might not bear the author's name, but the reader recognizes the vocabulary, the favorite stories, the tone, and the most common subjects of interest. Sometimes one can read a work and know instantly who wrote it because the style is such a signature of the author. That's why there are Hemingway and Faulkner writing contests in which parodies are such clear imitations.

If God is indeed the Maker, humanity can see a characteristic style and tone that runs throughout the universe God made, including the human intuition itself.[6] If God is indeed the Maker, creation should have a consistent and recognizable authorship. In the lines of our lives, we should hear the familiar tone of voice of an author we've read before, even without the author's signature. Akin to latent knowledge, this is deductive knowledge. It's another element of what you didn't know you knew.

The pages that follow will explore how the combination of latent knowledge that we pick up through daily experience and the deductions that can be made from it are sufficient to assure us not only that we have reason to believe in but also that we in fact already depend on God.

The Missing Piece

LOOKING FOR GOD IS LIKE the painful experience that a person may have when she puts together a jigsaw puzzle. Splashed out in an avalanche across the table, colored cardboard pieces slowly come together in a coherent image. She has a feeling of growing satisfaction as the mess becomes a ring of sense and structure and then slowly works its way toward an increasingly obvious conclusion. But at the last minute, something goes wrong. Neither the box, nor the floor, nor anyone's recollection can account for the location of the last piece. There is a gaping hole right in the middle of the picture of the sailboat or the flower or the Italian villa that stays open like a bully's laughing mouth. Now the puzzle is a disappointment.

I want to hone in on that hole.

There are two things that can be said for it. First, no one would dispute that something is missing, even if the puzzle came out of the box incomplete. Every element of that puzzle sitting on the table points toward the part that is elsewhere. The nothingness implies being. It would be absurd if the woman came to this point and concluded that the puzzle makers had decided to invent a picture with an intentional hole in it. She presumes that it is supposed to be a complete picture. She has a latent idea of how the thing is supposed to work, though the puzzle comes with no instructions.

Second, an observer would have a really good sense of what that missing piece would look like if she had it. She can deduce the colors, the contour, and the image that she's looking for. She can mentally complete the puzzle without actually having the last piece.

This is how belief works.

Holes in Our Reasoning

OUR WORLDVIEWS, which develop throughout the course of our lives, are like a puzzle that slowly comes together. An eighty year old has a panoramic viewpoint of which a sixteen year old is just beginning to catch a glimpse. Over time, we learn how to relate to one another, how to provide for ourselves and our families, how to adventure. We learn complex rules of social adaptation. We learn codes of ethics and means of coping. However, even at eighty, there are gaps in the puzzle. These holes are our missing pieces, and they're filled with implications.[7]

Daily living requires that we accept a vast network of assumptions and presuppositions that we cannot help but take for granted:

- We accept that our perceptions of the world around us are accurate and that our senses aren't playing tricks on us.
- We assume that there are real moral rights and wrongs to which people should be obligated.
- We assume that life has a purpose and that we play a part in that purpose.
- We assume that there can be meaningful communication in which two people accurately share what they are thinking.

There are fundamental beliefs on which we depend without much reflection. When a three year old asks a string of "why" questions, the parent takes a stab at the first few. Eventually, the parent is reduced to some sort of final, unquestionable foundation. The parent settles for "Because God made it that way" or "That's just the way it is." (I always preferred "Go ask your mother.") That last answer to the string of questions is a foundation, something that we assume without further explanation. Philosophers have given these kinds of ideas various names, such as "properly basic beliefs" or "foundational beliefs." For simplicity's sake, let's call them *assumptions*.

When we take a good hard look at those assumptions, we realize that they depend on something to ground them.

Those are just holes in our experience, and we are mentally filling in the piece we think should go there or assuming that piece can be found.

What I mean to suggest is that some sense of foundation has to exist or else much of existence starts to unravel. And that foundation is not simply a question mark.[8] We shouldn't treat ourselves like children and settle for a dismissive answer. Our foundational assumptions tell us a lot about what the foundation can and can't be. Not just any puzzle piece will fit in that space. The parent may settle for a God of the gaps when they are tired of answering. In this book, we'll see that the foundation for our most profound assumptions is no more a God of gaps than the resolution to this pattern: 1, 2, 3, 4 . . . is a "5 of the gaps."

A Couple of Holes

A COUPLE ELEMENTS of human experience draw us to ask some hard questions. They are both common and piercing. Few of us can escape the questions, "How should I live?" and "What happens when I die?"

Immortality

For instance, every culture in human history has taken some kind of guess at the nature of life after death. This, at a simple glance, is strange. There is no reason why human-ity should be inclined to the assumption that life doesn't end. There's no reason why biological life should ever develop a survival instinct, much less a survival instinct with a religious imagination. The most dogmatic evolution-ary biologist would be desperate to explain how a single-celled organism one day mutated itself into a longing for eternity. And yet, consistently across borders and ethnici-ties, humanity has cried out in unison, "That's a hole and something goes there!"

Consequently, cultures have come up with a vast post-mortem architecture for what the afterlife or the under-world should look like. Furthermore, they have then developed ethical systems based on those fantasies. "Because we are going there, we should behave here." Life is filled with a feeling of direction. We may disagree on what that missing piece is going to look like, but con-sistently over cultures and centuries, we seem to agree there's a hole right there.

If we step back from our assumptions and consider them in the light of day, we would have to admit that we have little basis for our beliefs about eternity or for the decisions we make about the purpose of life or even for the sense that life shouldn't just end. Those assumptions indicate a missing piece in our worldviews, something we casually and without thought fill in. Even confident atheists have a disquiet about their future forecast. They may well accept that they will return to the dust, but we rarely see them throwing parties to celebrate the fact. Human happiness is robbed by an unavoidable death, a reality of which we are all latently aware, though it rarely makes for pleasant dinner table conversation.

So here we have not a person or two but an entire species who, through the course of ordinary living, develop the common assumption that life shouldn't come to an end. I once sat down with a man who had spent his life operating on the assumption that at death, life dissolved into nothing. He was quite content with this worldview. To his mind, the issue was resolved. Until he had to bury his own daughter. At the moment of releasing the thing that gave his life meaning, he couldn't let go of life. Something deep inside him told him that life had to survive death. A naive reductionist would say that hope for the afterlife is just wishful thinking. But in fact, it's a universal conclusion. It's an assumption that everyone normally picks up along the course of life's way. And that assumption is a hole in the puzzle of life. Everyone comes to realize that they have been assuming life shouldn't end, and most of us function with the intuition that something should make sense of our assumption.

Morality

There is a second example of an almost universal assumption that has big implications. We have deeply held moral commitments, which, although socialized into us by parents, church, and community, seem to depend on something more than a social context. We use those same moral principles to turn around and criticize the parents, church, and community who gave them to us, implying that we all answer to something greater than social norms.

"Don't lie," I tell my daughter.

"What about Santa?" she asks.

And thus, we both believe in a moral standard bigger than the two of us, even though she learned it from me. I am not the source of the standard, merely its ambassador. There is some moral foundation out there that we have both intuitively agreed to—and acknowledge—though neither of us is prepared to explain in detail how we know it's there. What that greater something is remains a mystery, but we clearly depend on it. The need for moral foundation is a space we assume can be filled in. We know there is a piece that would make sense right there. Where that standard comes from is a hole in the puzzle. As the author and professor C. S. Lewis implied in the opening chapter of *Mere Christianity,* there is a universe of mysterious implication in the lunchroom cafeteria protest, "Give me a bit of your orange; I gave you a bit of mine."[9]

Most of us act as though there were solid grounding for our moral commitments. We assume something will come along and justify our sense of compassion for the oppressed and our indignation at the dishonest. Very few people would say that morality actually has no foundation and that moral commitments need not be taken seriously.

The same will prove true for other gaps in the puzzle of human experience. Someone needs to explain why we have a sense that we came from somewhere, and why we assume that people want to tell the truth, and why humanity seems wired for religiosity. We're latently aware of these unjustified phenomena, and we really believe there are missing pieces somewhere that legitimate our most profound presuppositions.

The goal of this book is to lay out in plain sight some of the most basic, universal assumptions governing daily living. We'll then have a sense for what pieces we're looking for. There is clearly something missing, something in the background undergirding human thought, something giving us reason for our assumptions. Rather than allowing it to remain a tangle of unexamined inclinations, we'll see if we have reason to trust our intuitions.

Instead of looking to physics or astronomy or anthropology or paleontology, we can find God by looking into the caverns of the human heart. As clearly and as quickly as the mind can fill in the image of the sailboat from where the existing puzzle pieces stop, we can fill in the missing pieces of human experience. The conclusion toward which they lead will be intuitively obvious. The piece that completes the puzzle of human intuition and experience is beyond the biological, the chemical, and the anthropological. Experience points us toward a subjective something that can't be reduced to the physical world. And that something may turn out to be a Someone.

How to Know What You Know

LATENT AND DEDUCTIVE knowledge play a part in the hunt for the missing pieces. Knowledge of the existence of God is not something that needs to be dug up in the library or a laboratory. It's something we've already picked up along the way. We've made all kinds of necessary assumptions based on a theological position we have taken; we just don't routinely stop to think about what we've assumed. This book is all about how to explore what we didn't know we knew.

The Pros and Cons

THE PERSON WHO SUDDENLY realizes something he already should have known may feel a bit embarrassed, the way Socrates' audiences often did. Socrates prided himself on exposing knowledge that his listeners already possessed. Through a series of directed questions, to which his two-dimensional listeners usually simply answered yes or no, he would show them that they could logically deduce new conclusions from what they already knew to be true. Sometimes this led to the flustering implication that the listeners should have already drawn the conclusions on their own. Usually it led to the conclusion that his listeners should have known better than to open their mouths to Socrates.

The Grecian philosopher was eventually put to death under official charges of corrupting the youth. Unofficially, he was killed for being annoying. It's mortifying to have someone show you in front of everyone else what you should have already known.[10]

Some people following the path of this book's implications won't believe in God simply because it means confession—admitting they were on the wrong track or missed the obvious. They go through their lives executing annoying intuitions. Nonetheless, people who can swallow their pride will find they already possess a sufficient knowledge of God, which they had overlooked.[11]

On the other hand, for those who can brave the humility, acknowledging that innate intuition for God is empowering. It's like a coin that turns up in your pocket only when you go digging through the laundry. It was already there, but it couldn't be spent until it was found. The owner only partially owned it. What if there were thoughts in your mind like the coin in that pocket? There is an awareness of God that is just as accessible as that lost coin; it's yours, but you don't have the power to invest in it until you find it among your things.

Or again, imagine someone finding, in a cluttered room, behind a piece of furniture, an electrical outlet. It's been hidden there all along, a resource to the power that runs every appliance in the house. Yet because the resident was unaware of it, it sat there functionally powerless. He had less power in that particular room, not because it wasn't there, but because he didn't know. It's hard to start your car with keys that you can't find. Some ideas have power. For the person who is uncertain about religious commitments, there is an idea already loose in his mind that is filled with power. He simply has to plug in.

Unlike other books of this kind, this one will teach you *absolutely nothing* that you don't already know (sorry, no refunds). But what you didn't know that you already knew will change (and power charge) everything.

Questions for Discussion

1. HAVE YOU EVER discovered something that you didn't know you knew? It might be something you had forgotten and later remembered, or something that you had intuitively picked up without realizing it. What was it?

2. WHAT DO YOU THINK of the Bible's claim that people are without excuse for not believing in God (Romans 1:20)?

3. DO YOU THINK someone could prove the existence of God? Why or why not?

4. WHAT ARE SOME of the primary reasons you think people choose to believe in God?

5. WHY DO YOU THINK people struggle to believe in God, rather than confidently affirming or rejecting him?

6. WHAT DO YOU THINK of the claim that some people make that faith is blind and cannot be established by proof or reason?

7. EXPLAIN LATENT and deductive knowledge in your own words.

8. IF SOMEONE ASKED you for the single best reason you can think of for believing in God, what would you say?

9. IF YOU WERE 100 percent confident that God exists, how would it change your life?

10. IF BY THE END of this book you are confident that God exists, are you willing to live out the natural implications of that conclusion?

For Prayer and Meditation

SPEND SOME TIME THINKING about the big questions of life that you've left unanswered. If you were to stand in front of God today, what questions would you want to ask him?

2
THE HARDWIRING

The Antennae

YOU MAY BE A reader who picked up this book maintaining a smug and aloof position: rational, heels dug in, and hard to convince—a good way of preventing yourself from being conned by every charlatan who rolls into town marketing a miraculous, new baldness-curing tonic. Healthy skepticism is necessary in a wily world. However, you may not be as objective as you think.

There are two images that can help us think about our skepticism, our objectivity, and our brains: a blank marker board and a GPS. Most of the history of Western thought has flip-flopped back and forth between similar images when describing the mind. The image of the marker board has dominated a lot of modern, Western history. It's the reason you may feel comfortable imagining yourself to be an unaffected skeptic. A marker board is static. It sits waiting for information. It's not committed. The information written on it is never quite as solid and dependable as the board itself. The information may come and go.

The rival image of the GPS describes an alternate way our brains might work. A GPS gives directions. It's active. When it receives information from a satellite, it's because it's trying to get you somewhere. Contemporary neuroscience tells us that our brains are in motion, hard at work, rather than sitting as passive recipients of information. The image of the GPS captures the sense that our brains are actually doing something when we learn and that we affect the learning process as we learn. Brains actually shape information as they take it in.

If our brains are truly blank marker boards, skeptical readers can justifiably sit back and doubt what they are reading. The problem is that the blank marker board of the brain has never actually existed.

Let's begin with our hardwiring. Let's start with the strange fact that our brains are not marker boards, but instead are groping, unsatisfied antennae. We are always at least latently aware of forces that guide our lives in many directions, rather than leaving us as objective observers. We may have never stopped to think about what all that motion means.

The Blank Slate

MANY OF US HAVE the idea that human beings are blank slates waiting to be written upon. It's important to realize this hasn't always been a popular viewpoint. There was a long season in human history when cultures understood humanity as spiritually intertwined with the world around us, and events in the physical world were seen as tied in a cause-and-effect kind of way to the state of our souls. Prayer caused rain. Likewise, we by and large believed the physical world around us was widely populated with invisible but very real spiritual beings.[1] Many intellects now think of this season as an intellectual winter, a time when human understanding was blinded by a flurry of bad ideas.

These same intellects saw the Renaissance and later the Enlightenment as springtime. We did away with souls. We did away with substances. We did away with tree spirits, totems, and talismans. Hard, objective particles rolled like an avalanche over the squishy and subjective spiritual realm. As science developed, Galileo stretched the cornea to telescopic lengths and bent it to microscopic precision. Everything worth studying was subject to the measurements of the human senses, and anything else was decidedly superstitious. Descartes disenchanted and Hume deconstructed.

Around 1690, John Locke published a work that would turn humanity decidedly in the direction of thinking ourselves to be blank slates, *An Essay Concerning Human Understanding*. In the essay, he said that we do not need God to implant knowledge about the world in the human brain.[2] The senses were all we needed to learn about the world, and the brain could just be a blank recipient. This marked a sharp turning point in the history of human thought. After that the eyes were no longer the window to the soul. Instead the eyes were the USB port to the hard drive of empty storage space: the blank slate.

The most skeptical readers come from these traditions. The problem is that the model of the passive brain does not resonate with either experience or neuroscience. Modern studies of the brain are just beginning to explore the way brains seek, store, retain, and flush information—and these studies show the brain to be anything but passive. Ongoing research shows the brain is an active agent in shaping information. You and I, witnessing events through the same pair of glasses, would not know the same thing, because your brain and my brain do different things with the knowledge. Modern philosophy is also now rejecting the idea of a blank slate.[3] The brain reaches out to grab at information, arranges it, puts it on certain "shelves" of the brain, manipulates it, and uses it in a multitude of ways. While your body may be sitting in an armchair with brows furrowed and arms crossed, your mind is not.[4] We tend to assume ourselves to be more objective than we really are. In fact, our brains point us toward certain kinds of knowledge.

We don't need neuroscience to know the brain works this way. An example from common experience illustrates that the brain is not merely a blank slate.[5] Two different groups of young adults were asked whether or not they were happy. One group scored significantly higher than the other group on their self-evaluations. The difference between the two groups is that one group was first asked, "How many dates have you been on recently?" before they were asked, "Are you happy?" The other group was asked the same two questions in the reverse order. Apparently their minds evaluated the second question in light of how they were feeling after answering the first. If minds were simply a blank slate, the information contained within them wouldn't be so slippery. Instead, we seem to shape knowledge based on how we receive it. Whether or not we've read a single page of cognitive science, we can tell from common experience that brains are active in the learning process and knowledge is shaped by mood and disposition.

Rather than a blank slate, the brain seems to have a mind of its own. If the brain has established directions before we begin driving it, where exactly is it going?

Following the GPS

I HAVE A GPS unit in my car, a Global Positioning System, which tells me where I am, where I should go, and how to get there. It even calls out directions in an almost-human voice when it comes time to turn. It's a woman's voice. We've known each other for some time now. We've become familiar with each other. She doesn't get mad when I question the logic of her decisions but instead calmly reiterates the route she recommends I take. Occasionally I will ask her to find somewhere to get coffee nearby, and she obliges. It's a peaceable relationship—except when I know she's wrong, and she won't stop talking, even though I already know where I'm going, and I didn't ask for help. Then I alternate between arguing with everything she says and drowning her out by singing along with the radio. The worst part is that sometimes I realize I've actually made a mistake and am heading in the wrong direction, but something inside me makes me afraid to admit it to her, for fear that she'll bring it up again next time we get into an argument.

The problem with my conundrum is that she is a machine. She's not going to change her mind no matter how I bargain or plead, because she does not have a mind. The GPS is simply hardwired to tell me where to go and how to get there, and it will always be hardwired the same way.[6]

We're far more like the GPS than the blank slate. We have much to gain from listening to internal directions. We don't need to wait for the slate to get filled up with correct information before making decisions about the purpose of life, because we're constantly being moved. Like a GPS, we are always pointed in a direction, and though we rarely notice it, the direction means everything. We can try to drown it out, but the hardwiring can't change what it has to say.

We are used to taking our hardwiring for granted and paying little attention to it. When people keep a promise, we rarely question their doing so, because we assume that at some level everyone should. Everyone's brain points more or less in that direction. When we hear of a culture that worships its ancestors, we don't usually burst into laughter, because anyone who misses a revered grandfather can see that it's hardly surprising that a culture might. That guy is being driven toward honesty, and those people are being driven toward the afterlife. The many broad assumptions governing our most important decisions go largely unquestioned, but clearly the brain is doing something more than recording information. It's looking for information. Already the brain has ideas about *how* the information is supposed to work. Our understanding of what is going on in our own minds is, in the words of one philosopher of cognitive science, "a mess," and it always has been.[7] So it is hardly surprising that we might have all along been receiving clear directions and missed them while we sang along with the radio. However, our seeking, directing, internal GPS tells us a lot about the course that life is taking.

When we turn our attention to the hardwiring, we find libraries of information and lots of intention. Finding God is merely a matter of listening to the internal GPS. The human heart is a God Positioning System. There have been many attempts in the realm of Christian apologetics to coerce the human mind. But effective Christian apologetics has always been a matter of liberating the heart.

That the human heart is always searching, never sitting statically as a blank slate, is the groundwork for belief in God. It's the most certain evidence that we can't resist belief.

Made in Motion

WE CAN'T SIT STILL. You think you're doing it right now, but you're actually on a racetrack.

The earth is rotating on its axis at around 1,000 miles per hour, depending on your latitude. Wonder why you feel tired in the morning? Look at how much ground you covered last night! Additionally, the earth is rotating around the sun at around 67,000 miles per hour. You're on an intergalactic tilt-a-whirl. Realizing this is enough to cause existential nausea.

Face east right now. Hold your hands up at ten and two. It's like you're steering the planet, eh?

Human beings are moving in a lot more ways than one. We are constantly moving biologically as well. We are born with all kinds of impulses, drives, desires, fears, appetites, and passions. We have an urge to feed, to procreate, to survive, to defend, to flee, to parent. Human life is directed in its very hardwiring. Most of these are involuntary, and most of them are hard to control. It's as though we were born on a conveyor belt. More important, the things toward which we are driven have critical implications. We are forced to make decisions that are drenched with value judgments. The desire for a juicy cheeseburger can be written off as a biological impulse with value-neutral consequences—not so much the desire to protect ourselves from our enemies.

We're moving sociologically. We have a desire to love and to be loved, to be understood, to have sex, to be coddled. We respond well to hugs and adversely to abuse. We seek out friendships. Piaget's studies of children show their proclamations are aimed less at meaningful conversation than at simply being heard.[8] We discover early on that we have voices, and we want to be recognized. The human personality, on the whole, runs narcissistic and dependent, and thus we are always headed desperately toward someone.

We couldn't sit still if we wanted to. Everything is in motion. It's in our hardwiring.

Thomas Aquinas decided that all this motion had to come from somewhere, that there must be a Prime Mover who started the movement.[9] This was one of his proofs for the existence of God.[10] I think that once we admit that we're in motion, it's hard to deny that there is a God, but for completely different reasons than the ones Aquinas provided.

The brute fact of our directed hardwiring, that which keeps us in motion, makes it impossible to ignore God. Here's why.

Unsure of Agnosticism

EVERYONE CAN SEE that humanity is in motion: biological, sociological, geographical, moral, and more. Neuroscience is merely confirming what everyone, including John Locke in his time, experiences every day: that our hardwiring directs life rather than allowing us to hang around like a blank slate. Now a balanced person might have some tolerance for the person who claims he can't tell what direction his life is moving, but not so much for the person who denies there is any motion at all. Yet there is a wide group of people who claim to be in the former group who actually fall squarely in the latter. As the roller coaster of life speeds by, you can hear them yell, "I'm not moving!" Agnosticism, or the claim to be unpersuaded by the evidence both for and against the existence of God, rests on the belief that the mind can sit completely still and consider evidence.

Agnosticism made the slow crawl into the public eye after being born from the philosophical viewpoint of the blank slate. The term *agnostic* popped up somewhere around the 1870s. Thomas Huxley is sometimes credited with coining the term,[11] but it seems to have been in the air at the time. Huxley combined agnosticism with newly minted Darwinism to reject Christianity. The term floated around, graduating from academic to popular literature when Bertrand Russell claimed it for himself and tried to pin down its definition in a 1953 publication.[12] It's a new word, in the grand sense of history, because never in human history has anyone actually thought that such a worldview might have credibility. The blank slate is still a relatively new idea.

To be precise, though, there are a variety of gradations within the doubt of God's existence, and none of them are sheerly objective. In fact, the variety of types of agnosticism shows how wide our biases can be. There are those who are desperate to find out if God is there, and there are those who are anxious about the consequences of God turning up, like a kid into mischief. There are those who are adamantly opposed to religion but who want to cover their bases by declaring a feigned, eleventh-hour neutrality. Some have a vague sense that their faith life has no foundation and no passion, but they are simply too lazy to investigate, so they remain sort of thinly religious. Some slates wish to be written on and some do not. Each of these groups claims the term "agnostic," when in fact they probably aren't on the same team.

Let's tweeze out one particular faction. There are those who will tell you they are only six-sevenths of the way to atheism. They won't get to *atheist* (from the Greek, suggesting completely opposed to the belief in the existence of God), but they don't quite stop at the more neutral, implied meaning of agnosticism (unable to make a clear assertion about God's existence, pro or con). They're sort of in-between. They are opposed to belief in all its forms that they've experienced or can imagine. They want to equate Yahweh with Zeus, as though all versions of faith were a hoax. However, they claim that actual atheism requires a mathematical certainty, and they won't go that far. We might coin a new term, also from Greek roots: *apistic*, opposed to faith. They have a will-to-disbelieve. They don't want it to be true, but won't clearly claim that will, hiding it in a feigned objectivity. They stop there between the rock of faith and the hard place of atheism and dig in their heels. So the agnostic is dependent on the claim that he himself is a blank slate, objective and unmoving, and any attempts to write on him have simply failed.

Most so-called agnostics actually camp out right there: wanting faith claims to be untrue but refusing to reject them entirely. They therefore claim to be objective blank slates, still waiting for more evidence.

However, given the hardwiring, there are two reasons why I'm not sure whether or not agnostics can actually exist at all.

First Problem: *Maybe* Isn't an Option

THE CLAIM TO AGNOSTICISM won't hold, at least not for long, for the very reason that humanity is in motion. The *apistic* claims to remain poised and unmoving in between two options, belief and nonbelief, each of which has a fierce draw on him. At the same time there are multiple forces in his life pushing him to make a decision about going in one direction or another. He is being both pushed and pulled at the same time.

Imagine a kayaker who is on a river adventure and injures herself. She races desperately to reach medical assistance, but comes to a fork in the river and doesn't know which route is correct. She can't very well put on the brake at a fork in a rapidly moving river while she tries to decide which way to go. The force of the river won't allow her to hesitate for long. And given that she needs to get where she's going, she can't wait forever.

Or imagine a group of children challenging one another to try to stay poised near the top of a slide at a water park. Jets of water push from one direction, gravity pulls from the other, and it's slippery. They are more likely to be entertained than successful.

The demands of the human heart and the call of human life keep humanity in all kinds of motion, having profound ramification on the moral principles to which we adhere and the purposes for which we live. By living, people necessarily make a statement about life. A lifestyle is a team jersey.

For one, biologically, human beings are hardwired for relationships, and we begin reaching out for them from the crib. The relationships that we form are wrought by value judgments. Secondarily, we are psychologically constituted to seek meaning and purpose. Something makes us believe that life is valuable. We have a vast architecture of legal systems that quantify exactly how valuable life is, and we go looking to protect its value. Also, we are physiologically in motion, predisposed to fear and desire. Because of this, we naturally embark on certain pursuits. Something drives accomplishment and survival; neither is value-neutral. Additionally, we have an ethical inclination that makes us hunt for moral clarity, and we get stuck in situations that force us to make ethical decisions. And then, finally, the reality of our deaths comes coupled with a longing for immortality. We are being pushed and pulled at the same time in all sorts of ways. All of these demands require some crucial decisions about what life is for and where it is going. "Our hearts are restless," Augustine observed.[13] The GPS keeps calling out directions.

The apistic looks at all this motion and yawns. He wants to be a blank slate. This is fundamental to the evaluation and ultimate rejection of agnosticism: agnosticism depends entirely on the assumption that humanity can sit in a state of unfazed objectivity. If in fact the human mind is irreversibly in motion, then we are constantly in the act of making decisions based on an assumption about what life is for. I doubt that we're ever agnostic. Latently we're aware that we've been pushed and pulled into situations that require us to think about the purpose of life.

Aristotle put it this way.[14] A human being standing equidistant from both food and drink is not going to die of both dehydration and starvation due to an inability to decide whether he is more hungry or more thirsty. Sooner or later, impulse and drive will take over, and he'll go for one of them. Jean Buridan, the French political scientist, was satirized for claiming that a human being faced with two equally good moral choices could not make a decision. The image used to ridicule his theory was a mule that could not starve to death poised between two equally delicious bails of hay.[15]

The apistic feels the drive for purpose and meaning and love and morality and order. He can turn and embrace a divine reason for his existence, which answers his deepest needs, or he can deny God and leave port for stormy seas on the vessel of self-reliance. Either way, he's not going to sit there and starve for lack of meaning and purpose. He's going to go looking for it one way or the other. Life is short. The decision can't wait.[16]

The human heartbeat is a launch-pad countdown. It is only going to beat a certain number of times, and at each second that count drops by one. Eventually it will reach zero and the count will stop. While we may ignore it day to day, we can hear the pulsing count in our ears. Saying that we don't feel we have enough information to decide doesn't stop the countdown, and sooner or later that pulse is going to make us take our best guess, with or without certainty. Life is lived from the perspective of a vast network of decisions already made, thus obligating us, and a wide range of decisions still lying unavoidably ahead.

In this world, people fall in love, divorce, bully, flee, discover, sink into depression, seek justice, procrastinate, and wake up in the morning longing for something different. Life is a waterslide, and we may be able to choose which way we fall, but we don't get to choose to sit still. The atheist philosopher Jean-Paul Sartre admitted as much when he said of someone who has a difficult moral decision to make, "he cannot but choose a morality, such is the pressure of circumstances upon him."[17] Circumstances force us into a moral position of some sort, and thus a position that exposes what we really believe about the universe.

Agnosticism in any form isn't a lasting option. It's more like a momentary wavering before one acts. It's a hesitation or a deep breath. It's that instant of weightlessness when the airplane hits a turbulent bump, and everyone hovers a quarter inch above their seats before the angles and vectors and forces bring them all back down again. One can be an agnostic for about that long.

Ultimately, the apistic has already started to make a decision about God, despite denials on his part. He either lives with a conscience that tells him he's going to answer for what he does in life, or he doesn't. He either lives as though life is valuable or that it is not. He lives from the perspective that life comes from nowhere or that it is designed, and that it is headed somewhere or that it simply erodes.

Imagine someone who behaves as though his life has lasting value and should be lived morally and conscientiously. He's already started to give up on agnosticism. He's already started to make a decision. This moralistic agnostic is really just a nervous, would-be believer. He's the kid who sits in the back seat of the car complaining that he hates his family as they go on vacation together. Ultimately, he's simply protesting a commitment that he is already making. They're his family whether he likes it or not.

An amoral agnostic, on the other hand, someone who really lives as though he will not answer for anything he does in life, has the second problem on his hands.

Second Problem: *Maybe* Isn't an Excuse

THE APOSTLE PAUL WRITES in his biblical letter to the Roman church that there is enough evidence of God's existence in creation that people are without excuse for their disbelief (Romans 1:20). Likewise, Jesus, after an apparent miracle failure on the part of his disciples, scolds a faithless (*apistos*) generation and proceeds to heal the person whom they could not (Mark 9:19). A sound scolding for lack of evidence doesn't quite make sense. Because the Greek term Jesus uses for the disciples is *apistos*, "against faith," he's likely holding them accountable for choosing not to believe rather than for not having enough data. They are a "faithless" generation, not a "knowledge-less" generation. They know miracles occur because they've already seen a few. Clearly the biblical voices sing this song in unison: there is enough that's clear about God for humanity to believe in him. People who claim they don't know aren't off the hook.

Maybe the apistic has a courtroom drama going on in her mind. Most likely due to a Judeo-Christian hangover, she envisions a day in eternity where the God of all creation says to her, "Why didn't you believe in me?" And she can say, "I didn't *not* believe in you. I just didn't have enough evidence to be sure." And the Lord will say, "Oh, sorry, my bad."

There is a general assumption that neutrality implies a lack of liability. It's the ultimate Get Out Of Jail Free card. Perhaps this springs from a childhood full of the passive voice: "I don't know how it got broken." Perhaps it comes from an adulthood numbed by news reports of political figures saying, "I can't remember what was said." Either way, the assumption is that if we claim we didn't know, then we can't be held accountable.

Couldn't or Wouldn't?

In the same courtroom, ignorance only means immunity when the ignorance cannot be shown to be negligence. Not knowing is not the same as avoiding knowing. People are only off the hook when they can show both that they didn't know and that there was no way they could have known. However, they are still guilty if they didn't know because they avoided finding out.

If the apistic wants to claim that he isn't intentionally avoiding God, that he isn't being negligent, he has to demonstrate two things: the absence of obvious information and, just as important, the inability to sense the need to search for information. That is to say, the answer can't have been sitting right in front of his eyes, nor could he have sensed the obligation to go find an answer.

The first one is obvious. A person is not negligent for failing to help a colleague who has injured himself getting out of the bathtub in the privacy of the colleague's own home. The person was not aware of her colleague's fall.

However, she might be held responsible if she should have checked on him when he didn't show up at the office for three days. That second issue confronts agnosticism. God has not opened up the clouds and in a booming voice announced, "Case settled." Therefore, apistics assume, they are not responsible. However, if, as we will see, there has been a gaping absence of God with all indications pointing to a place where God should be, those apistics are still responsible for having failed to go looking. They are pretending that the artist designed the jigsaw puzzle with a hole in it. If all of life's motion is pointing us toward a decision about value, morality, and eternity, the doubtful are still culpable.

Negligence is exactly what's at issue in that heavenly courtroom. Jesus and Paul hold humanity responsible for latent knowledge intentionally disregarded. Because humanity is in motion, it can be held accountable for not looking where it's going. A driver who closes his eyes on the freeway can hardly say in his own defense, "But I couldn't see anything."

Besides, the claim to lack information in the Information Age is odd at best. Clearly, there is enough information to live on, enough to nourish and sustain humanity. The onus is on honest agnostics to produce a pretty substantial bibliography of failed research.

The Fool's Heart

THIS MAY BE THE SOURCE of King David's name-calling when he writes in the Hebrew Scriptures, "Fools say in their hearts, There is no God" (Psalm 14:1; 53:1). Rather than a mere taunt, there is profound content to the accusation. Ceasing to believe in God is an overt rejection to the direction in which life is moving, and the word for "fool" is deeply interwoven with the idea of life's movement.

The Hebrew word for fool that David uses is *nabal*. It can be distinguished from other Hebrew words also translated "fool," which tend to mean something more commonplace, like "silly." *Nabal*, on the other hand, is harsh. It shares the same root as the word for the withering of plant life.[18] The word is used for leaves that wither (Psalm 1:3; Isaiah 1:30, 34:4, 64:6; Ezekiel 47:12), grass that withers (Psalm 37:2), and flowers that wither (Isaiah 28:1-4; 40:7-8). Fools are those who have cut themselves off from life, are dried up, and are about to disappear for lack of nutrients. Fools are those who are deteriorating toward death, wilting.

David may not so much be casting insults as making an observation about living things. Withering things say in their hearts there is no God, because when we say there is no God, we intentionally cut ourselves off from the source of life. Without the source of life, motion slows. We begin to erode. We begin to dry up. The withered one has said in his heart there is no God and then stops thriving.

A Deduction

AS HUMAN BEINGS we have a latent awareness we were born into cycles of decision making and obligation that have profound implications. These cycles require us to make commitments about the value of life and the basis of morality. Action is a commitment. Largely the knowledge that we are caught in passionate, life-changing decisions sits unnoticed, because it is in fact the norm for everyone, and yet everyone still manages to spend a lot of time watching TV. Still our immersion in a moving world carries with it the implication that there is no such thing as a lasting "I couldn't decide, I was watching TV."

Admittedly, this doesn't lead to any clear deductive knowledge about God. But it does lead to a clear deduction about ignoring God, specifically, that it can't be done. To exist is to commit.

Overcoming the Blank Slate

FOR MANY, THE PRIMARY challenge to the quest for faith is not some scientific data that must be explained or philosophical question that needs to be answered. Somewhere in the modern era skeptics got the idea they had the right to evidence that they could get their hands on. They had to be able to take pictures of it, put it on a scale, or dissect it into slices that would fit under a microscope. Until evidence was presented, they could safely sit back and ignore the issue. Taken at face value, this is an absurd requirement. None of the things that make human life valuable or interesting can be tested empirically. When we talk about the meaning of life, we mean purpose, heroism, love, ethics, and beauty. The physical universe is at best an awe-inspiring soil from which the real stuff grows. Insisting that that which is most valuable must also be tangible is nonsensical—if for no other reason than that the very claim that you have to be able to get your hands on evidence before you believe is itself a claim for which there is no evidence that you can get your hands on.

No one is a blank slate waiting for proofs to be written on them.

Seeking God means putting aside the obstacle of overly stringent criteria for what qualifies as evidence. The criteria we use to live in wise and healthy ways are sufficient criteria to apply in the search for the source of wisdom and the standard of health.

I once encountered a woman who felt like she had every reason to believe in God but refused to do so. There was one particular obstacle to her believing. She said she was afraid of making a commitment to which she couldn't hold herself. To her mind, choosing to believe in God required an unflinching commitment to constant obedience. The slightest wavering or doubt on her part, she thought, would nullify the validity of the original commitment. She felt she shouldn't make promises she wouldn't always keep, even a pledge to believe.

In her anxiety I heard a kind of passion for truth that I respected and even kind of envied. She wanted to have real integrity in her commitments. On a whim, I asked her if she planned to get married one day. She said she did. So I asked, for the sake of comparison, if she would be pledging never to let another man catch her eye, never to snap at her husband at the end of a long day, and never to take up a hobby that would steal weekends away from her marriage. People often make covenants and commitments without expecting that the spirit of the obligation will be perpetually heartfelt. Yet the fact that commitments require persistence doesn't mean that promises are illegitimate, only that it's hard to keep them. She seemed to think she could get married without a promise of an effortless romance, but somehow she had decided that commitment to God came with a different set of requirements.[19] Belief in God springs from the same passionate and risk-taking movement that gives life to romantic love.

Secondly, what I liked best about the woman's thinking was that she had a deep sense that things like promises were valuable and should be honored. I told her that her integrity actually made God's existence all the more likely and all the more appealing. Rather than being nervous about whether or not God will accept our commitments, wasn't it great, I asked, that the author of faithfulness might plant in us a desire to be faithful?

Our conversation put her at ease. What stood in her way was not a God who is inaccessible, but a misguided anxiety about what it means to believe, an anxiety she never directly thought about. She assumed she could remain an intellectual blank slate when everything in her life pointed toward decisions she was already making. To her credit, her hesitation showed she had the clarity to take the decision seriously.

The human heart is hardwired toward the God that is on the move. It forces humanity into decisions that reveal the need for God. God and the lost soul are like lovers who have sensed each other from afar. One is clear-sighted, direct, and intentional. The other is blind, wandering, and hesitant. But they were meant to be together, and they are both moving. God has wired us to take promises seriously, and he himself is waiting to enter into promises with us. We were made to reunite with him, and he is waiting for the GPS to guide us, like a father standing by the window waiting for a lost child to come home.

Questions for Discussion

1. DO YOU BELIEVE you can trust your intuition like a map or a GPS to guide you toward God? Why or why not?

2. WHEN HAVE your intuitions proven trustworthy? When have they been wrong?

3. WHY DO YOU think some people find it difficult to believe in God?

4. HAVE YOU EVER used the word "agnostic" to describe yourself? When and why?

5. DO YOU BELIEVE that people can remain agnostics throughout the course of their lives?

6. READ ROMANS 1:18-22. Why might people be held accountable for what they do or don't believe even when they claim not to have enough information?

7. READ PSALM 19. In what ways might God's presence be visible in creation?

8. WHY MIGHT PEOPLE prefer to say they are not sure about God rather than to reject him entirely?

9. WHY MIGHT PEOPLE feel hesitant about saying they are certain that God exists? Is there any reason you personally do not feel you can say that?

10. HOW WOULD YOUR LIFE change if you realized that most of the things you live for depend on the existence of God?

For Prayer and Meditation

THINK ABOUT THE TIMES you have been least sure about God's presence in your life. Picture the consequence of a life lived without making a choice if in fact God is actually there waiting for you to decide. Set your mind to clarifying where you stand.

3

BELIEF ON THE BRAIN

Hardwired for Commitment

THE REASON THE TERM *agnostic* was not created before the modern era is not because inhabitants of the modern world are brighter than the populations of former eras. It's because never before in the history of the world has humanity been inclined to define the concept of permanent uncertainty. Instead, most of humanity has believed, and despite recent decades of formalized, popularly accepted skepticism, the world goes on believing.

Atheism has already made its best case for itself, and there is really no new information for which it can wait or hope.[1] Every new archeological find further substantiating biblical history is part of a growing body of evidence. Atheists have nowhere left to dig and nothing to dig for. Realizing they cannot successfully persuade the vast majority of humanity to stop believing, they are grasping for alternatives. Therefore, the modern era has come up with agnosticism. Agnosticism is atheism on life support.

Given humanity's inability to sit still, we've consistently chosen to move in a certain direction. People make concrete decisions about what life is for, where it comes from, where it ends, and what should be done in the meantime. The choice of direction is a profound statement about the way the world is made. It says a lot about the hardwiring. Where humanity has always chosen to go is in search of something supernatural.

Why that search begins is a curious thing. The standard skeptic attributes the religious instinct to the psychology of ancient people that somehow got wired into the genetic pool. The faithful believer might say almost the same: God is somehow written on the heart. Either way, there is a growing consensus that we are biologically religious.

Epiphanies

AS OPPOSED TO MERELY waiting for evidence like a blank slate, here's where the path toward God actually begins. Humanity is wired for motion. In the course of traveling through creation, God's pseudonymous novel, human beings pick up latent signs of the Creator. We get a sense for his style and tone. We start to pick up on his themes. We see gaps where only God could go. We are full of latent information.

Now it often takes a catalyst to direct our attention to the latent ideas that we've been holding on to. There are moments when people have a brief inclination that something, or someone, is out there. People with whom I have spoken about it have had a moment when the grandeur of nature or the crisis of a near death experience or a moral wrestling has made them suspect the possibility of the supernatural.[2] These moments come without explanation.

Some people dismiss them and some people embrace them, but everyone will know what I'm talking about. It's that instant in which we get a sense for the latent knowledge we've been carrying around. Suddenly we suspect there's something we've been missing and some part of us we haven't noticed before.

These moments are catalysts running throughout human experience that are meant to serve as triggers for belief. They are trip wires for the skeptic and booby traps for the unconvinced. They are those instances when we are suddenly and unavoidably aware of knowledge that has previously been lying quietly in our subconscious, now awakening a gnawing in the gut. They do what a glimpse of a succulent steak does to a person who hasn't realized it's an hour past lunchtime. Suddenly they draw our attention to things we've previously taken for granted or ignored.

Usually these are branded generically as "religious experiences," but if we dissect them properly, we'll find that what they are is a sudden piercing discovery of something we have been unknowingly carrying around with us.

Many people don't see them as such and in fact oddly insist that they've been looking everywhere for proof of God's existence without finding it. In reality, those very people have been doing everything they can to tiptoe through the land mines, usually by applying stringent criteria for finding them. They're so hard to avoid. C. S. Lewis commented in his autobiography that an atheist "cannot guard his faith too carefully," because there are signs of God lying around everywhere.[3] There is no doubting that these experiences occur.

The process of intelligent analysis of what the experience was, what triggered it, and why it happened should produce more than a wistful pause.

What we know in common experience has actually been observed by the most profound minds in the fields of psychology and anthropology. William James started to analyze these experiences of faith in his studies of religion.[4] He noted that there were certain states of consciousness that were different from normal, waking thought to which he couldn't help but ascribe metaphysical significance. That is to say, there is a difference between a daydream and a whisper. A daydream can come from a mixture of boredom, caffeine, and the firing of synapses in the brain. But if one were to daydream about a dragon, it would be silly to leap off the couch. That daydream came from inside, not outside. However, if one hears a whisper, it's best to turn around; it came from someone else. There are experiences like whispers that should make a people who are staring at the material world look over their shoulders. Whispers come from somewhere else.

Unfortunately, James had the cards stacked against him when he proposed this theory, in that he was an American lecturing to a European audience in 1902, which, to the European academics of the day, had the distinct feel of a teacher trying to listen attentively to a kindergartener's show-and-tell. Freud's take on James is patronizing. Perhaps because of his humble hesitation, James went no further than to suggest that we have an awareness of our finitude and a sense for a greater infinity, and we are only at peace when we credit that nebulous infinity with more worth than we finite creatures ourselves possess. Nonetheless, James named that there are "experiences" that allow people to enter through the doorway of the religious life.[5] We may be afraid that our common experiences would be dismissed by sharper minds, but the sharpest of thinkers have had the same experiences and made the same observations. The hardwiring is so obvious that it doesn't take an academic to see it, and yet it's so essential that an academic can't avoid it.

These epiphanies awaken in us an awareness of things that we've noticed in the course of human experience, things that point to something beyond the normal, material world. We largely take them for granted and ignore them. However, these religious experiences draw our attention to things we've left undisturbed, like teachers pointing to a spelling error in a student's paper and clearing their throats. The implication is that we should have noticed a hole in the puzzle. Once we reconsider the missing pieces, we can start to deduce the place of God in human life.

These experiences exist to divert attention off of the material world, which is immaterial, and onto the immaterial, which actually matters.

Neurotheology

THE REASON WE HAVE epiphanies is because the brain is wired for them.

Throughout most of the history of the world, in most cultures, and even for most individuals, belief in a supernatural world, spirits, ghosts, and divine beings has been the norm. We've hardly been agreed on what to believe in, but we've agreed on believing. That has to do with a hardwiring for religiosity. It's not a superfluous choice; it's a much deeper instinct. The passions of the human heart, the gravity of our finitude, and the drive for meaning have set us in motion toward belief. Then the brain actually points us toward religious belief.

When the shadow of a hawk passes over a newly born baby chick, the chick runs for cover. It does this instinctively and without training. Likewise, when humanity is confronted with lightning and lava, earthquakes and thunder, we run for cover. It's an instinct that comes without training or forethought. We may project simplistic explanations onto ancient cultures that created pantheons of gods, but what we interpret as simplistic rationale was actually something pre-rational.

James would say that the religious instinct is foundational to humanity. There are too many experiences that incline us in the direction of the supernatural to assume they are either false or limited to certain individuals. We all have the sense for something greater than ourselves. However it is deconstructed or articulated, it is nonetheless a nagging feeling that we have. We could say that there are certain hard facts about humanity: we have skeletons, we have skin, we reproduce, and we're religious.

In fact, contemporary neurobiology confirms a link between religion and biology. The hardwiring literally points toward God. Neurotheology[6] broke onto the public scene in the United States at the beginning of the millennium. *Newsweek* once ran a cover image entitled "God and the Brain."[7] The ensuing article described "the brain's spirituality circuit" which is a hardwired, biological, materialistic foundation for religious experiences. There had been studies that required MRIs of praying nuns and injections into meditating monks. While the research is in its infancy, it suggests that the brain reacts in certain ways to religious stimuli.[8]

Humanity has always taken all of this motion to be leading somewhere, and in fact the motion of human life won't allow for anything else. God created the brain to point in his direction, like the magnetized North Pole on a compass. Sociobiologist E. O. Wilson observes that religion feels "full and rich; it feels somehow *right*." Furthermore, he says, "The human mind evolved to believe in gods. It did not evolve to believe in biology."[9] While he finds nothing necessarily supernatural about it, he concurs that religion is not only psychological but also biological. *Time* proclaimed in 2009, "our brains and bodies contain an awful lot of spiritual wiring."[10] The piece said that physical health is likely even improved by religious belief. This has led naturally to speculation about a religious gene.

The GPS points us in the direction of God. All of the motion in the world pushes humanity in that direction. Simultaneously, the brain responds to religious stimuli, as though the outer world and the inner world were pushing in the same direction. This is not in and of itself a proof of God's existence, of course, only the direction in which humanity has always moved and is continually inclined to move.

Superstition

WE MIGHT NOW look to putting aside the obstacles that stand in the way of our following our inclinations and explore this biological religious instinct for what it is. There are two such obstacles.[11]

The first is the general dismissal of religion. The "enlightened" Western approach to the religious instinct is to brush it aside. Cicero claimed that the word "superstition" derived from the Latin "superstitiosi," meaning "survivors,"[12] because parents who wanted their children to survive became overly dedicated to prayer. Since then, "superstition" has been the dismissive branding that modern minds have used to rule out the possibility of religious claims, as though belief was the frail daughter of fear. This, however, divulges a less than scientific predisposition. A true scientist would come up with a round of experiments to poke and prod at the instinct.[13] A scientist would be as open to the chicken coming from the egg as vice versa. Those who casually dismiss faith as superstition must establish that the need for God causes belief in something that is imaginary. It might be rather that the God who exists makes humanity need him. God is not necessarily caused by the brain's wiring; the brain's wiring may be caused by God.

For example, in his study on architecture, De Botton assumes that his instinct toward worship is a psychological effect of religious architecture. He writes, "Touring the cathedrals today with cameras and guidebooks in hand, we may experience something at odds with our practical secularism: a peculiar and embarrassing desire to fall on our knees and worship a being as mighty and sublime as we ourselves are small and inadequate."[14] What's at odds with his practical secularism is not the rafters of the sanctuary, but simply a dedication to secularism that ignores other cues and clues. He's chosen it before he's tested the alternatives. The dead giveaway is his embarrassment. His self-consciousness about his own religious instinct is proof that he wasn't interested in being practical anyway. Pragmatism would require attentiveness to the obvious: we have an innate sense for God, and that instinct could come from any number of places, only the least likely of which is vaulted ceilings. Embarrassment is what one feels when the external voices of peer pressure are stronger than the internal voice of common sense.[15]

Rather than causing delusional religious fantasies, things like magnificent architecture, panoramic seascapes, and the vast celestial canopy are merely speaking to the religious instinct. The religious instinct is a sonar, constantly sending out signals and listening for a response. We hardly need to be embarrassed when something pings back.

Atheists have wielded the term "superstition" as a snobbish weapon, the playground bully's pointing finger that depends on power rather than intelligence. Rather than branding the religious instinct, we might better go at it like scientists and assess its true nature. The GPS is pointing us in a direction. That instinct is meant to awaken us from our materialistic slumber and make us look for something more. The obstacle to our belief here is simply a modern, narrow-minded prejudice against religion that prevents us from looking objectively at the ubiquitous religious instinct. Rather than a fearful hope clung to like floating debris after a shipwreck, the religious instinct is hardwired, and rather than brushing it aside, we ought to examine it. Again, this is not to say that it is proof that God exists, only that a scientist is responsible to entertain the possibility of God's existence,

A friend of mine is an astronomer and an atheist. In one of our several conversations in which we'd locked horns, I asked him, "Have you honestly never even prayed to God that if he was really there that he might reveal himself to you?" My friend laughed and confessed that he had. He said that one afternoon he was sitting on his bed contemplating the possibility, and he spoke to a God he wasn't sure was listening, asking for something just like that. He said that at that moment, the clouds outside parted and suddenly his room was filled with sunlight. He said that it made him laugh, because he realized it was just a coincidence. The one whose love language was the stars dismissed the God who knew how to speak to him. If superstition is the blind clinging to unsubstantiated beliefs, I would say my friend held to a very superstitious atheism.

A Second Obstacle

IN THE FACE OF A universal religious instinct, the doubtful like to point to the plethora of religious options as an insurmountable obstacle to the particular claims of any one faith. How could someone choose to be a Christian when there are Muslims, or Mormon when there are Catholics, or Buddhist when there are Baptists, and so forth? The conclusion is an implied assessment of the religious instinct: that it points nowhere because it points everywhere.

The most naive apistic thinks that a flippant "What if you're wrong?" is enough to dismiss every faith. The religious instinct is remarkably indiscriminate on matters of doctrine. We are born in motion, and we choose a direction to go, but there is very little about the instinct itself that guides the choice. To return to the kayaker at the fork in the river, she may have no choice but to pick one tributary or another rather than endlessly waiting, but if each tributary stretches beyond sight, the river itself can hardly tell her which one leads to safe harbor and which one leads to a waterfall. Thus a religious instinct may only leave us in anxious movement down a dubious path. For some, the answer to this problem is that no paths can be viable.

However, the fact that someone can make false faith claims doesn't dismiss the possibility of a real God any more than an error in subtraction renders mathematics impossible. One waterfall doesn't mean that all branches of the river lead to a crash. Some claims are simply wrong, but it would be senseless to conclude they must all be wrong. Not all faith claims are on the same footing.

This is easy to see. The sane can agree that religious suicide bombers have got it wrong, whereas humanity generally agrees that broad ethical codes like "Thou shalt not murder" have got it right. People by and large are willing to admit there are false religious ideas and true religious ideas. The fact that there are a lot to sort through hardly renders them all impossible.

Some choose no paths; others take them all. The instinct to avoid distinction between religions is largely fueled by a wise conscientiousness about the history of religious warfare. Understanding that scarred past, people are drawn toward tolerance. It seems offensive and elitist to suggest that only one faith could be right above all the others. However, we hardly call a man prejudiced for walking into a pharmacy and insisting that one medicine is right for his particular malady over all the others. In fact, it would seem quite odd for him to say, "In the name of tolerance, I accept them all as equally viable." That guy might well end up attempting to remedy his tuberculosis with an aspirin.

So the multitude of religious faiths renders them neither unilaterally invalid nor all on the same footing. In fact, there is a far more plausible explanation for the diversity, and any anthropologist studying the religious instinct should see it.

A Few Guesses

If, throughout human history, people have been wired to search for God, one could hardly be surprised that history would have produced a variety of results. In fact, it makes perfect sense that pioneers of the religious inclination would explore new religious alternatives—that some would pray to the trees and some would offer incense to the sky.

We should hardly be surprised that somewhere back in time the instinct toward hunger took someone from eating plants to eating meat. It's only a step further to get to eating cooked meat. Only a touch further would be combining food to create seasoning. And eventually, whether one is a committed Catholic or a hardened evolutionary biologist, we can see how an original, vague instinct toward hunger finally led to beef stroganoff, clam chowder, and jam. The instinct itself didn't choose what finally got eaten. In fact, it didn't have much say in the matter. It only pointed prehistoric consumers in a direction, and then they guessed at what might be best to digest. There were likely a few who tried poison.

The religious instinct has led to a lot of guessing. Rather than disproving the possibility of the existence of God, the diversity of guesses (and the similarities between different and even conflicting faiths) actually makes it all the more likely that God is there. It confirms that the hardwiring points in a direction.

A Deduction

AGAIN, THE AIM HERE is not to prove the existence of God, and no proofs have been offered. This is simply an exposition of the natural instincts that have existed throughout all cultures and throughout history, which have over and over again led people to God. This doesn't prove that he's there. It does, however, rule out the feigned attempt at neutrality known as agnosticism, the flippant charge of superstition, and a lukewarm Christianity that avoids the distinctives of world religions. A humanity designed by God that turns out to be hardwired to go looking for him should hardly surprise anyone.

The existence of multiple and even contradictory religious claims does not mean either that they are all acceptable or that none of them are. It doesn't mean the religious instinct cannot be trusted. It merely means the religious instinct is a force that pushes humanity past agnosticism and indifference. Historically it has pushed humanity to all kinds of guesses. Regardless of their accuracy, it's clear that human beings are hardwired to begin the search for God.

This alone doesn't prove one answer true, but it does prove that there is a question that needs answering, which cannot be reasonably neglected. However, there is another instinct guiding us further along in our exploration, another something we've noticed before and to which we need to take a moment to pay attention.

Questions for Discussion

1. DO YOU THINK everyone has a religious instinct? Why or why not? Do you think everyone at some point or another wonders about the existence of God?

2. WHY DO YOU THINK cultures throughout human history have developed beliefs about the supernatural?

3. IS IT POSSIBLE that so many cultures could have had religious instincts if there were no God? How easy do you find it to believe this?

4. DOES THE FACT that the religious instinct leads to so many different religious faiths and doctrines make it hard to believe in anything?

5. HOW WOULD YOU respond to the question about whether or not the existence of false religious claims makes all religion suspicious?

6. HOW WOULD YOU respond to the question about whether or not the existence of many religions should imply that they are all equally viable or that they all lead to the same conclusion?

7. AT WHAT MOMENTS in your life have you felt most inclined to think about God? What makes you trust or distrust those inclinations?

For Prayer and Meditation

THINK ABOUT THE MOMENTS in your past when you have been most inclined to believe in the existence of God. Remember the things that pointed you in his direction.

4
ABSOLUTELY

God, Our Father

BEING HUMAN IS FUNDAMENTALLY an act of parenting. Even for those who are never biological parents, we are a generation giving birth to a generation. Everything we create is done so with a mind to legacy, and everything we conserve is done so with a mind to longevity. Everyone who recycles is a grandparent. All of our genetic matter, our civilization, our science and our philosophies are on a mad race from our parents' hands, through our fingers, and on to our children, like a baton being passed between relay runners.

Parenting is part of the GPS, and parenting is fundamentally a microcosm of divinity—that is, it points toward a heavenly parent. Being a parent myself has done a good deal to help me see how I'm wired.

There is a season in my household in which all four of our birthdays fall within a two-month span. That means there are ten months of the year in which we are in a birthday cake desert. For ten months, buttercream frosting is a memory thinly spread over expectations for next year.

This last year in our home, there came a day when my family was out of the house for the afternoon, and I saw that there were only two pieces of birthday cake left. For the year—two pieces left for the year! It was at that moment that I got fairly philosophical. I thought to myself: it is a father's job to protect his children from all harm, and there are all sorts of things in birthday cake, like sugar and fat, that are bad for children. It is my job, I thought, to protect my children from anything that could hurt them.

When my family arrived home, they looked anxiously from the chocolate ring around my mouth to the empty plate and back again. And I realized, looking at their crest-fallen faces, that my family does not appreciate how much I do for them. I had completely fallen on that grenade and no one even said thank you.

Now an evolutionary biologist will say that the inclination to protect one's young is a simple manifestation of the survival instinct. It runs throughout the animal kingdom, and it is anything but religious. It is the fundamental drive of selfish genes to preserve and replicate themselves (though this biologist never exactly explains on what basis he anthropomorphizes genes, giving them wills and desires).

However, there is a part of parenting that cannot be attributed to anything but an intentional hardwiring, and that is the moral tutoring of our children. Moral tutoring of children requires parents to stand on a foundation of something that exists outside the material world. It is the indication that we are made to believe in something beyond ourselves. We latently know that there is some basis from which we are teaching morality and some essential reason we are doing it, but we are capable of teaching morality without self-reflection.

A skeptic could dispute that moral training is just a form of social adaption that allows children to function well among their peers. It could simply be the most basic form of preparation for communal living, a necessity of the survival instinct.

That kind of explanation is strained on two levels.

First, predisposing our children for moral living only suits the goal of survival up to a point. Parents tell their children, "Never tell a lie." They rarely coach, "Don't tell lies, unless you know it's to your best advantage in that situation, and then lie." The absolutism of our moral coaching does not come with the anticipation that our children will later on develop a more nuanced worldview in which they themselves will come to determine that lying is in some cases appropriate. We actually mean for them not to lie. A mother is not proud of a son who grows up to be selectively dishonest based on a situational ethic. Moms are proud of sons that everyone knows are good to the core, even at a cost to themselves. The morality that we teach to our children is not a kind of functional socialization; it's based on a belief in the innate value of human beings and the innate value of morally upright behavior.

Second, the view that the moral training of children is evolutionary and based on survival makes even less sense when one thinks about what is actually required to survive. In fact, one author put his hand to codifying the principles necessary for a little prince to grow up safely in the world, and The Prince looks like anything but the common conception of moral tutoring. If survival is what is at issue, morality should largely be naturally selected out of existence. Even apistic Stephen Jay Gould describes "the vexatious problem of altruism—previously the greatest stumbling block to a Darwinian theory of social behavior."[1]

Wired for Absolutes

WE PARENT WITH AN EYE for absolutes. Our goal is to teach children that some things are ultimately right and some things are ultimately wrong.

Situational ethics are not the goal, even though most everyone operates from a perspective of situational ethics. In fact, we tend to correct situational ethics out of our children. When children make excuses for misbehavior, they do so on the basis of a certain context. They say, "Well she hit me first," or "Papa let me do it." They seem to, at early stages, develop the sense that there might be some plausible reconstruction of the facts by which it will prove to have been permissible to do, in this particular situation, something otherwise not permitted in normal circumstances. "You let me do it yesterday," they will claim about staying up late, which is exactly why they cannot do it again tonight. However, to their minds, you have already opened the door to situational ethics by violating the bedtime yesterday, and if it's one thing that children know how to do, it's exploit loopholes. One should wonder about the need for law schools once you've seen the cunning of a five year old. It's exactly this behavior that parents try to close in on with their absolutes.

In fact, morality without absolutes is senseless. Morality without an absolute is like a race that has no finish line. Without it, the point of the race is lost and the race may as well be abandoned entirely. The absolute is exactly the standard against which all the exceptions are rendered. Morality without absolutes would amount to little more than announcing one's personal preferences. Without us ever contemplating it, the GPS points us in the direction of absolute morality, a fact of which we are all latently aware.

Think about the alternative. In a world without moral absolutes, no behavior could be ruled fundamentally wrong.[2] The best one could hope for was that they would be ruled distasteful or unpopular or, on some irrational basis of public consensus, illegal.[3] For example, rape could never be said to be morally wrong, only unpopular or hurtful. In fact, if one were to argue that morality were fundamentally just a construct of the survival instinct, one would have every reason for insisting that rape used to propagate a particular gene pool, for instance, is genetically advantageous. If morality were simply a part of the biochemically produced conscience, our conscience should not be prohibitive of rape.[4] In fact though, morality comes from somewhere other than natural selection, and such behaviors are rightly considered morally reprehensible.

If in fact we are wired for moral absolutes, we seem to be wired for something that could not exist in a universe without God. Without God, we are accidental products of time, chance, mutation, and natural selection. We are particles bouncing around meaninglessly in the universe like sand swept off the beach in a breeze, and we die in a way that is no more meaningful than the wind discarding dust. Without God, absolute morality has no cause and no place.

What would be left in a humanity without God is the most utterly narcissistic, megalomaniacal self-indulgence. It would be the survival instinct and nothing else. Voltaire is credited with telling someone to keep her voice down when they discussed atheism for fear that the servants would steal the silver. That's because without God, everyone would decide what was best and most advantageous to their own survival in any given situation. What would happen if all morality was reduced to utilitarian calculations in any given situation would be, in a word, hell.

Which, as a side note, has always confused me about the move to say that a good God would create some alternative to hell, or, perhaps, will in the end leave hell empty as love wins the day. This is confusing to me, because I've never understood hell as a cage. Quite the opposite, I suspect hell has no walls at all. Hell is not a constraint, but the ultimate liberty. And rather than a place where one is subjected to torture, again I suspect quite the opposite. Hell would be the one place where there is absolutely no discipline at all. Hell is humanity left to its own ends. Imagine this world with the final removal of the subconscious inclination for absolute morality, left with a population content with what's best for now and to most of us. What would a world look like where people agreed that their purpose was only survival?

For there to be definitive moral values, there must be something that makes sense of the dust. There must be something binding particles to purpose either by design or an ultimate evaluation at the end.

Again, this is no proof of the existence of God, which may begin to make readers wonder why they have gone this far in the book (still no refunds). This is simply to observe that we are hardwired for inclinations that cannot be filled by anything *but* the existence of God. Nothing in the material world will fill this longing or explain our parenting. It's a gap in the puzzle. It does imply, of course, that resistance to belief in God may be more of a will-to-disbelieve than a true intellectual hang up.

Invaluable Values

IRONICALLY, SOME OF GOD'S best friends at this point are the atheists. When atheists produce their litany of complaints that they claim led to their rejection of God, they usually at some point do so on moral grounds. They turn to the Bible and criticize genocide, sexism, and the vanity of a being who demands worship. They protest, on moral grounds, God's character. However, it's at exactly this moment that they are borrowing the referee's rulebook to protest that the referee isn't following the rules. They want to claim that he is so far off from the rules that the referee must not actually exist. But from whence comes the rulebook? The very fact that the atheist has an absolute moral groundwork to say that God is completely wrong cannot come from the material world. If, as atheists must claim, humanity is an accidental byproduct of time, chance, mutation, and selection, they can hardly point to some moment along the way, when, just between that zygote and that single-celled organism, morality occurred. There's no point on that continuum where life evolved from senseless matter into something of ultimate, unquestionable value. Right and wrong don't grow legs and crawl out of the primordial soup. Be clear here: atheists aren't saying they don't prefer God's behavior or they wish they had more power than God. They are appealing to ultimate, unquestionable, absolute values that God has violated.

Many noble atheists hold determinedly to social values allowing for the moral critique of God. They oppose slavery, the degradation of women, war, and the death penalty. They are not anarchists. In fact, many of them are legalists. But any review of the history of law will show where laws are grounded. The unalienable rights with which we are self-evidently endowed come from our Creator, says the Declaration of Independence. Without a founding purpose, we have little basis for claiming a right to life, liberty, or happiness.

Jeremy Bentham, a militantly anti-religious atheist, called the idea of natural rights "nonsense on stilts."[5] His only standard for rights are those that are advantageous to society. When it comes to slavery, for instance, he says it is not acceptable because a greater number of people are hurt by it than helped by it. However, here he shifts from the language of "advantage" to the language of "good" and "evil." He co-opts moral terms to try to give his pragmatism a stronger edge. But there is no fundamental basis for objective morality in his system. Principles and practices of society are not absolute. They can be given away when they are no longer of practical advantage. He even goes so far as to say on practical considerations that he cannot argue against one master owning one slave, because neither represents a majority, and thus society might be advantaged by slavery.[6] On this, some of the American founding fathers just knew better and were more humble. They included a brief but essential grounding for their values.

When someone does not believe in essential moral values, we don't usually respect it as a rational and alternative worldview. We usually diagnose it. A person dispensing with social norms surrounding work ethics, law abidance, and honor codes, would be classified as having an antisocial personality disorder rather than gaining respect as a free thinker.

Evolving out of Morality

MORALITY AS A MERE PRODUCT of a survival instinct makes little sense if we take natural selection seriously. The process of natural selection is ingenious: something in nature mutates and creates a new life form, then the forces of nature themselves sit like Caesar over the new gladiator who has been thrown into the coliseum to decide whether to give that mutation a thumbs up or a thumbs down. The one who gets to live has babies and creates more of itself. They then have kids who have kids, and so on, until another one mutates and gets thrown back in the ring. The process continues, favoring traits that best help the lineage to survive.

Now, if natural selection actually works, a few million years should make for some pretty shiny, strong, effective gladiators who have good teeth and rarely catch cold, which, for the average person who walks around the mall and looks at this pinnacle that humanity has reached, should make us wonder what Caesar was thinking. Specifically, there are some traits of humanity that should by all means have been weeded out by now: sleep (which makes people vulnerable to predators for a third of their lives), self-consciousness (which is essential to despair), endoskeletons, appendices, wisdom teeth, birth defects, stupidity, and obesity.

And, of course, profound moral obligations. Moral obligations lead to monogamy and even celibacy, which are not the fastest route to propagation and survival. Moral obligations lead to self-denial, which is almost the exact opposite of survival. Rather than aiding survival, absolute moral values are at best a speed bump.

The Cosmic Babysitter

SOME HAVE ACCUSED theism of being the parental means to hiring a cosmic babysitter for the moments when the kids are unsupervised. Again, the charge has already made a chicken-and-the-egg commitment. It is just as rational (and as wise) to say that God has created humanity to parent because he himself is a parent, rather than saying that God the Father is the product of a child's imagination. Again, it would only make sense that the natural instincts of a created humanity would point them in the direction of a Creator, more so than that the instincts themselves created the Creator. A GPS doesn't cause people to dream up a fictitious mapmaker.

Freud makes this misstep in *The Future of an Illusion*.[7] He asserts that God is merely the projection of humanity's need for a powerful father figure to watch over them after the universal discovery that biological fathers are flawed and limited. Freud may well be right that the deep longing for a healthy and strong father figure inclines people toward a belief in God, but again, that does not dispel the possibility of the existence of God. It only makes it more likely that the designer programmed the creation to find its satisfaction in him. Plus Freud fails to account for the fact that a moralistic, powerful, heavenly father figure may not be all that appealing to most people. That image doesn't exactly warm your heart. The image feels judgmental, which explains why a conversion and bending of the will would be essential to believe in God the Father. I kind of wonder why the guy who credited humanity with the Oedipal Complex, which involves patricide, would also imagine that God was invented as an object of paternal comfort.

In the end, if God is indeed some kind of cosmic babysitter, it might not be because humanity dreamed him up. It might be because we were made by a parent.

The Parenting Instinct

THE INSTINCT TO PARENT is at the heart of humanity's hardwiring, regardless of whether we marry or stay single, give birth or remain celibate. In our hearts we perceive ourselves to be at best a relay runner who holds in our hands a baton of the entire future. In the course of our lives, we perceive ourselves to be the potential bearers of precious cargo. This is why philanthropists leave their names on plaques and grandfathers are proud to have grandsons with the same autograph. Coupled with that instinct is a deeply held inclination to adhere to and pass on an irrefutable moral foundation.

Ultimately, my children have a deep sense of the level to which I want them to aspire morally. When I think I might have caught my daughter in a lie, she knows how to offer a final word in the conversation.

"Are you telling the truth?" I ask her.

She looks at me with determination and answers, "Absolutely."

Questions for Discussion

1. WHAT WOULD THE world look like without God? What would it look like if every human being decided in unison that God did not exist?

2. WHY DO PARENTS teach their children moral values?

3. WHAT DO YOU make of the accusation that humanity invents moral values as a matter of survival?

4. WHY MIGHT SOMEONE deny that human beings have a desire for absolute moral values?

5. CAN YOU THINK of reasons why a committed atheist would hold on to absolute moral obligations?

6. WHAT DO YOU make of the accusation that the idea of God is simply a missing and made-up father figure who will watch over humanity?

7. WHAT DOES THE EXISTENCE of universal moral values tell you about humanity?

8. WHAT DOES THE EXISTENCE of universal moral values tell you about God?

9. IMAGINE A WORLD in which everyone lives morally. What appeals to you or does not appeal to you about that image?

For Prayer and Meditation

TAKE A MOMENT TO DWELL on the things in life and in this world that you know are wrong, the things that spark in you a kind of moral outrage. Think about how it would feel to face these evils in light of the stark reality that morality doesn't actually objectively exist. Picture a world in which objective moral values were clear to everyone.

5
COMING AND GOING

Of Monkeys and Men

HUMAN BEINGS SEEM less prepared for survival than primates. A primate goes through life pragmatically, thinking toward the next meal, safe journey across the clearing ahead, what will result from wandering away from the tribe. They rarely, I suspect, wake up feeling depressed that their best days are behind them. Their attention looks to the future rather than the past. Human beings invest as much or more in looking backward as in looking forward. We amass genealogies, we interview grandparents, we have blood tests that trace our lineage, and we ponder cosmologies. The future is a bit more hazy, and we approach it with an attitude that falls somewhere between panic and idle speculation. Good strategists are actually a rare breed. To many people, they are mystics and prophets.

Our instinctual search for a past, or a source, is something we take for granted. We are latently aware of our own curiosity. We rarely stop to look at that curiosity and wonder why it's there, as opposed to only looking forward. The hardwired rear view is, as we'll see, a thoroughly religious inclination.

And Now

WORSE STILL, WE SEEM to have hardly any orientation as to what time we are in right now. Humanity has come unstuck in time, to misuse Vonnegut. There is an odd experience we have when we look at a nephew and say, "Look at how big you are! It seems like just yesterday!" There is a more petrifying moment that occurs when we are forty and, half-dressed, accidentally pass in front of the bedroom mirror. The turmoil comes from the inner sense of youth that seems to have gotten dislodged from our bodies. We don't naturally feel the age that we are. I've heard a ninety year old look in a mirror, baffled, and quip to himself, "How am I this old?"

This is because we are not hardwired for mortality. Our deepest instincts tell us that we are on a different timeline than the one we seem to be on. We were created to be eternal beings, and the aging process is something that takes us through the emotional experience of our bodies molting away from our souls. People look in the open casket at the wake and think, "That's not her." Whether we will own up to it or not, we know an empty skin when we see it.

The intuition we casually dismiss or accept as mundane is actually a megaphone heralding eternity. It's God's voice speaking into the material world with absolute clarity. We've picked up along the way the impression that somehow aging is all wrong, but that idea sits latently in our minds, sheathed. I remember the moment I watched my father lean over my grandmother's hospital bed and close her eyes for the last time, and at that moment I stopped brushing this reality aside. Everything we take for granted about aging and death is wrong. We're supposed to be shocked at exactly the moment many people shrug.

We've all had that experience where we see someone we haven't seen in a long while and notice that they've changed. If it's a child, the change is all the more pronounced, and we're all the more amazed. We could rightly wonder why that is. There is a latent awareness that aging feels wrong, but we simply accept and put up with that dissonance. Human beings who are amazed by time are kind of like fish being amazed by water. We exist in time. We're in it all the time. It should be pretty ordinary. A fish doesn't notice water, I suspect, because it was made for it. We notice time, I think, because we weren't made for it. We were made for eternity, and everything temporal ultimately jumps out at us as surprising. We have midlife crises because all of a sudden we are forced to say, "Wait a minute! None of this feels right!" And indeed, it isn't.

Consequently, we start to wonder how all this came to be and exactly where it's going. Time now becomes a matter in question. When did it start and when will it end? How much time do I have? Can I get more? Could I make it go on forever? The sudden attention to holes in the puzzle makes us wonder what might fill them in. We've had a latent knowledge that something needs to go there.

The Rear View Mirror

HUMANITY'S FASCINATION with identity is widespread. It's another element of the hardwiring that indicates how we're made. People research genealogies and like to tell stories about a family member several generations back whom they've never met, with pride for a family member's accomplishments. We feel a twinge of guilt when we discover that someone to whom we were related left his wife or owned a slave or went to jail. Genealogies are not entirely indifferent.

The search is more pronounced for the adoptee who goes looking for birth parents. There is a longing for some piece of identity that seems to be lost, even with a lifelong history in a healthy family, even if the person has no memories of a family of origin. Yet the search is far more passionate than a mere gathering of data. The search hurts. Again, there is no reason why human beings evolved out of the mud would develop such an emotional connection. The connection is not to a person, since the person in question has never been met. The emotional connection is to one's identity.

There is a corporate curiosity about origins. National Geographic has sponsored "The Genographic Project," an opportunity for people to take a cheek swab and mail it in for testing to determine their ancient lineage. The test promises to "reveal your deep ancestry along a single line of direct descent (paternal or maternal) and show the migration paths they followed thousands of years ago."[1] It is information pragmatically irrelevant to daily life, yet it has gathered an international following.

Whatever this longing is, it is yet another signpost. It is another catalyst making one suddenly aware there is a missing piece to the puzzle. There is something back there needing investigation, and while we hardly know why, some internal positioning system keeps pointing us in reverse.

Now there are two solid options of which I'm aware.

The first is that we came from the ooze. Billions of years ago, there was nothing, and then stars and space, and then lightning and amino acids, and then ooze. From the ooze came a sensitivity to light that turned into eyes, and flagella that turned into fins. Through Caesar's oversight of the mutations eventually came brontosaurus and bedbugs and bus drivers.

Now the bus driver is the most amazing of all. She has all kinds of fascinating, highly evolved traits, like a high-pitched voice and the ability to sneeze. Plus she makes the bus go. But her essence is the same as that of the ooze. It has the same value as the ooze, because value is not a step in the evolutionary chain. It's an attribute given by her community, but it is not so much a part of her as, say, her liver. When she dies, she will return to the ooze. And there will have been nothing in between but highly evolved ooze with a curious inclination to stare in the rear view mirror.

That is one option.

The other option is that we came from something that knew how to make sense out of ooze, something that programmed the ooze with purpose and intention and a destination. In this scenario, the value of the bus driver is of an entirely different kind. If she is no longer able to drive the bus, her value has not gone anywhere, because it doesn't come as a commendation from her community. It's somewhere a little closer to her liver in this scenario, in the sense that it is internal and cannot simply be removed (it is perhaps more essential to her than her organs). In this scenario, she was given value, because something destined her to a certain time and place for certain reasons that will in the end be assessed.[2]

Now these are the two options. The problem is only one of them is actually possible.

Stars and space coming to be out of nothing isn't exactly a simple thing. In fact, we know of material things that they never actually spontaneously pop into existence. Matter doesn't just come to be. Not ever. To insist that this is possible in one and only one instance, and *that* being the creation of the universe, is a bizarre kind of voodoo—a large leap of faith. There is no instance in which matter ever just appears, and the person who claims to be able to make matter appear usually comes with a bunny rabbit and magic wand.

Every material thing that comes into existence has a cause; there are no exceptions.[3]

The drive to look backward into our history and into our origins points us toward an awful gaping hole in the puzzle. We have on our hands a beginning that couldn't have been. Not long before the ooze, nothing was, and ooze doesn't grow out of nothing.

Atheism of the Gaps

I WILL NOT HERE entertain a third option, namely that the first option can be complemented with the idea that somewhere along the line in the evolutionary change, somewhere between lizards and birds, say, life all of a sudden developed the characteristic of having value. This view seems to me on its face absurd. It is the artificial insertion of exactly what the atheist needs in order to hold on to atheism while ignoring the hardwiring. This is, at best, a partial admission on the part of the atheist that he sees the same hole in the puzzle that the believer does. Something needs to ground our moral instincts, our sense that there is real value in life and things that should be held precious. Whereas the believer simply points over his shoulder to the place he came from, the atheist must insist that moral value simply is, as sure as the color yellow just is.

This makes for a ferociously funny turning of the tables, an ironic morality of the gaps.

The Front Windshield

NOW GIVEN THE REALITY of our mysterious beginnings, we may well nervously turn and look in the other direction. Perhaps on the other end of the line we can find something more stable upon which to anchor ourselves.

However, here again we are immediately confronted with the reality of the ooze. Upon our deaths, our synapses stop flashing, our bodies decompose, our bones may harden into something memorable if they are not ground to dust, but most of us float off into the wind. We are consumed back into the mess of matter that makes up the world.

Now if the mystery of creation gets written off as a curiosity, the mystery of death produces somewhat more anxiety. Fear of death is universal. Essentially every mortal is in the constant act of begging the prayer of Gethsemane. Jesus prayed in the Garden of Gethsemane that he would not have to suffer death; even those who do not believe in him know that longing. Humanity does three different things to deal with the ubiquitous finish line, all of which are forms of denial.

Looking for Everything

First, people try to eat the world before the world eats them. There is an unnamed intuition that we should try to take in any and all of life that we can, because the time will come when we are allowed no more and the ground will finally take us in. Eat, drink, and be merry, for tomorrow we die is the cheer of mortality (Ecclesiastes 8:15). Or as Heschel more articulately put it, what we lose in time we make up for in space. When we realize we are on a limited time span, which will eventually run out, we instead try to expand our borders to prove that our existence in this world was significant enough to warrant consumption.[4] We spend money because it makes the most of mortality and proves that we were worth being spent upon. I've always thought it ironic that we print "In God We Trust" on the back of God's leading competitor.

All of this is, of course, denial. No amount of making merry will add an ounce of value to the dead and the dust. It is the blind following of impulses. But how curious that humanity is so wired for enjoyment that we'll keep looking for it even when it would be pointless to find it.

Looking for Something

The second way in which some people avoid the reality of death comes when they live as though they might find purpose if they keep looking for it. It has been the aspiration of some of the desperately self-conscious to live as though life had purpose without the least anticipation that there would prove to be a reason to do so.[5] If one has no reason to believe that life has purpose, the search for purpose is irrational. But that person has a deep, innate sense that meaning *should* be there exactly where he's looking. At least this person is not denying that there is a fundamental impulse toward meaning that he can't escape. At least he's admitting to the fact that there is some sort of hardwiring that is overpowering the manual controls.

This person goes on searching for the missing piece. He is sifting through the ooze for meaning. He is looking through debris for structure. He has a sense that something should be there where it doesn't appear to be, a hole in the fabric of existence.

One study showed that people presented with good and bad photos always fixate longer on the bad ones.[6] People who learn bad stuff about someone else remember it more than the good stuff. People are more likely to bring up negative events in their lives than positive ones. Studies show that there is no exception to the fact that attention to the bad is consistently stronger than attention to the good.

Having read this, I can't stop thinking about it, which I guess is another data point for the study.

Rather than assuming we're just pessimists, though, I think we're seeing another way our souls show themselves. We're hardwired for perfection. Anything less than that, albeit ordinary and common, attracts our attention, because it stands out as odd, in the same way aging stands out as odd to eternal beings. A lamppost in the woods would only look odd if you're from a world where lampposts appear on streets. Life without meaning looks as wrong as a lamppost in the forest. Meaninglessness doesn't go there. Cracks and fractures are interesting especially if you're from a world where things don't get broken. Tears are provocative, especially if there's a world where they might be wiped away.

Hugh of St. Victor, a theologian of the early eleventh century, wrote, "When we admire the beauty of physical objects . . . we experience a feeling of tremendous void."[7] Beauty is a photo of eternity, and we go looking for beauty even when we think the world is finite.

So in this second scenario, the seeker looks around at an apparently meaningless world and realizes something doesn't feel right. She goes looking for something better when there is nothing to suggest that she'll find it, except the gnawing feeling that she should.

Looking for Nothing

There is a third option, which is worse, though it makes more sense. It's called fatalism and involves turning off the GPS. This third scenario denies the call of latent knowledge and the intuition that provokes the search for purpose. It faces head-on the reality that life is meaningless. Camus suggested, more whimsically than realistically, that the question of suicide was the only viable one for a world that had thoroughly embraced atheism.[8] Most people are not so dramatic, favoring suicide by lifestyle. It is the descent into depression and survival. When all that life consists of is the survival of the fittest genetic matter, there is nothing to do but survive. Here the whole becomes the sum of the parts. The parts are biological matter seeking to last longer, and the whole is a person who has nothing to do but keep the biological matter in "everlast" mode. Rather than finding meaning in and passion for eating, drinking, and merriment, instead they just age. In this world "all birth was but the prelude unto death, and every cradle swung above a grave."[9]

Beginning and End

HUMANITY IS WIRED to look into its own origins and destination. We are unavoidable extensions of our memories of yesterday and hopes for tomorrow. We long to know where we've come from and where we're going.

The Greek word for end is *telos*. Telos is a philosophical term that means the thing for which something is designed. Aristotle would say that the telos of an acorn is an oak tree.[10] It is that which it is designed to become, and the telos is somehow implanted in it and steering it toward its final destination. It's the blueprint of what a thing is to become.

To this, Jesus makes an interesting claim: he says that he is the beginning and the end (Revelation 21:6; 22:13). The Greek word for beginning is *arche*, and it sometimes has the active sense of the one who begins things. It could be translated *beginnor* if there were such a word—*initiator*. From it we get the word architect, the one who begins things with a plan.

It is as though Jesus were a sculptor carving a sculpture of himself: both the Creator and the image of what creation is to become. The architect *and* the blueprint. If humanity looks backward to the beginning of all things, the claim that Jesus makes is that humanity will see him there. And if we look forward to where we are going in the end, Jesus claims we will see him there as well.

Of course, those are just the claims Jesus makes. There is no explicit, empirical proof in human experience that assures us in advance that Jesus knows what he is talking about. There are only gaps into which that claim sensibly fits better than any alternative.

Again we see our GPS pointing us to look in certain directions. We have been carrying around a latent sense that we should be finding purpose in a world that doesn't necessarily produce purpose. There should be something starting us off and something at the end of the road.

Questions for Discussion

1. HAVE YOU EVER felt surprised at your age or at how fast time passes? Why do you think that takes us by surprise?

2. WHAT WOULD IT feel like to be an eternal being who suddenly realized it was trapped in a temporary body, a body that would die?

3. HAVE YOU EVER looked into your family history or genealogy? What do you think makes people want to know where they come from?

4. WHAT ARE THE possibilities for how the universe came to be?

5. HAVE YOU EVER wondered what the afterlife might look like if there is anything there at all? What do you imagine?

6. ARE YOU AFRAID of death? Why do you think people rarely have casual conversation on such a major issue everyone faces?

7. WHY DO YOU THINK humanity is inclined to speculate about the beginning of things and the end of things?

8. WHAT COMFORT IS there in believing that life had a purposeful beginning and is being drawn toward an intentional destination?

9. WHAT ARE THE CONSEQUENCES of believing that Jesus designed us in the beginning and that we will meet him again in the end?

For Prayer and Meditation

PICTURE A WORLD IN which you are created with purpose and design and intention. Imagine coming to the end of your life and discovering it all had reason and value. Savor this.

6
HOW EMBARRASSING

Telling On Ourselves

THERE ARE GAPS IN the human experience, and while we don't pay much attention to them much of the time, we are vaguely aware that they are there. We long for moral foundations, for an identity, for a purpose, and for someone greater than ourselves to make sense of our mortal lives. These presumptions motivate us to live morally and purposefully and even religiously. But none of this proves there is a God. This could all just be the happenstance and confusion of evolution. The fact that hunger makes us long for food, which satisfies hunger, does not mean that religiosity, which makes us hunger for God, will lead us to a God who satisfies our spiritual longings. None of this has been proof.

However, there is one element of human nature that makes a case for the Christian story. In fact, it's inescapable. It comes from a behavior deeply wired in human behavior. I've seen it even in early childhood.

When my daughter was a little girl, she one day came downstairs to breakfast with a markedly crooked hairline.

"What happened to your hair?" her mother exclaimed.

"I don't know," she said hesitantly.

"Did you cut your own hair?" Her bangs hung at a definitive, forty-five degree angle.

"I don't know."

"How do you not know?"

"I don't know," she said, and now I could see her try-ing to straighten the look on her face into the smooth, unaf-fected veil of innocence. She raised her little eyebrows so as to convey that she was surprised as her mother was. You could see one eyebrow really clearly.

"Are you saying that someone snuck into your room in the middle of the night and cut your hair?" the prosecuting attorney asked.

"Maybe."

We rarely tell on ourselves. Pride and shame run deep. From a very early age we feel the sting of someone laughing at us.

My son, who is younger than his sister, is not yet quite so sophisticated, but the feelings are the same.

"Did you color on the wall?" I ask him.

He puts an index finger to his chin like a philosopher and looks out the window, in case the answer might flutter by. "Hmm," he speculates.

You can see the tears beginning to form along the perim-eter of his eyes like the flick of silver minnows in a stream.

"It's okay," I tell him. "I just need you not to do it again." I hug him as he begins to cry.

We have a deep-seated resistance to embarrassment. It comes without explanation, and perhaps without rea-son, because when people can laugh at themselves we call them well-adjusted. The person who is embarrassed seems momentarily weak and exposed. But we all feel it.

Scholars have made some deductions about the human inclination to avoid embarrassment. Historians say that if an ancient story exposes the weakness of the storyteller, it's probably true. They call it the "criterion of embarrassment." It's the idea that given the chance to go back and rewrite history to make ourselves look better, we probably will. Therefore, the stories that are most embarrassing, particularly to the storyteller, are likely to be true.[1] We do anything to get out of telling on ourselves.

That little piece of hardwiring leads to some fairly supernatural conclusions.

Embarrassing Hero Stories

TO HAVE A SENSE for how embarrassing Jesus was, we have to have a sense for what his people had been waiting for. They weren't looking for a strictly religious figure or a teacher. They wanted a king.

Their hopes were based on the stories of a heroic king of long ago: King David. The highlight of all of Jewish history came when they ruled over their own land with their own king. The fact that the kingdom has slipped out of their hands into civil war and eventual conquest was their greatest shame. And after their kingdom falls, all hope is placed on a king in the line of David.

The Old Testament is actually a cliffhanger. The camera pans back from an empty throne, over Jerusalem's walls, to a bird's-eye view of a kingdom that is waiting for a king to come. The New Testament picks up in exactly the same place, except now the camera is panning in, past a star, past shepherds keeping watch over their flocks by night, to a throne that had been deconstructed and reassembled as a manger.

Everything in Jesus' life shows how strong their expectations were, as a few instances indicate. When Jesus fed five thousand people with bread, they tried to make him king by force (John 6:15). They did this because they had been ruled by another king, Caesar, who had conditioned them to "bread and circuses." James and John asked to sit at Jesus' right- and left-hand sides in his kingdom (Mark 10:37). In other words, they wanted to serve as vice president and secretary of state. When he rode into Jerusalem for Passover, their Independence Day, they wanted him to depose Herod, so they sang his praises. And when Rome realized what the disciples wanted, they put a mock crown of thorns on Jesus' head, a purple robe on his shoulders, and a sign on his cross stating "King of the Jews." When he rose from the dead, the only question on their lips was, "Are you going to restore the kingdom to Israel now?" (Acts 1:6). Everything in Jesus' life pointed toward the expectation of a king. Their vision for what he would look like was shaped entirely by King David. They were waiting for someone else like him, even from his bloodline.

Here's the rub. This is where the natural tendency to embarrassment becomes a factor. If a first-century Jew were going to make up a Messiah story in the first-century world, the story would look like the story of King David. He would certainly have in mind only the framework of a powerful national leader. He wouldn't make up a story that would contain details that were embarrassing to a political leader.

For instance:

- They wouldn't have him born to an unwed mother in a barn and a father who wanted a divorce, because that is anything but majestic.

- They wouldn't have included two different genealogies that don't immediately synchronize.

- They wouldn't have Persian Zoroastrian magi visit him, because it then looks as if someone else's religion got it right.

- They wouldn't have Herod kill off the two year olds, a virtually superfluous story that makes it look like God doesn't know what he's doing.

- They wouldn't have him baptized by his cousin, because baptism served to wash away sin, and his baptism makes it look like their Messiah had done something wrong.

- They wouldn't have him get in blistering arguments with the respected religious leaders of his day, because these leaders' endorsements are the kind needed by a king.

- They wouldn't have him disrupt the Temple, which would be as scandalous as the president throwing a fit in church.

- They wouldn't include a story of Judas.

- They wouldn't have him drink.

- They wouldn't mention prostitutes.
- And they certainly wouldn't have their hero nailed to a tree, which was a sign of disgrace (Deuteronomy 21:23).
- They wouldn't have the first witnesses to the resurrection be women, whose testimony was not as respected as a man's would have been.
- They would not have had him ascend to the skies; they would have had him ascending to some kind of earthly power.
- They wouldn't have left behind four accounts of his life, which at points seem to run along different chronologies.

All that to say, the story of Jesus is far too embarrassing to the main character. There is no way that advocates for him would have made up a story along the lines of the one we have. The story is in desperate need of some editing from a public relations representative. It would have been so easy to clean up the story to make Jesus more kingly, and yet he fails the criteria for kingship in almost every way.

Thomas Jefferson tried to fix the story.[2] He published a version of the Bible in which he removed the supernatural elements. These were the parts that unnecessarily imported superstition into what Jefferson considered an otherwise decent book of moral teachings. The result is a much thinner version than the original, one in which Jesus is reduced to the respectable position of a Socratic or Confucian wise man. While a first-century editor might have different aims and a different end, the Jefferson Bible gives some indication of what one could do with a story whose details don't fit the hero's ad campaign.

The problem with the story of Jesus is that it isn't a proper messiah story. A first-century Jewish person would listen to this story and rightfully ask, "Wait a minute, where was the Messiah in the story?" No one could have made it up. And in two thousand years, no one has come up with a plausible alternative explanation for why such an embarrassing hero story came to be.

God-Shaped Vacuum

BLAISE PASCAL SAID THAT there is an infinite abyss in the human heart.[3] In fact, that's not where the vacuum is. The vacuum is located in a tomb somewhere close to Jerusalem. Nature hates a vacuum, and people have been trying to fill that particular vacuum throughout history without success. They've been trying to put naturalistic explanations in the place of the story of the resurrected Messiah and failed. There has been no adequate explanation for why a hero-story, a messiah-story, a God-story would involve a tomb. Gods don't die.

Bertrand Russell naively asserted of the Resurrection, "We can't know that much about it."[4] In fact, we know everything we need to know. No one would make up such a completely embarrassing story that is so wholly out of line with the plot thus far.

In the ancient myth of Sisyphus, the trickster is condemned by Zeus to push a boulder up a hill. When he comes close to the top, the boulder's weight overwhelms him, and it rolls back down to the bottom. Sisyphus is condemned to try again ad nauseum. Skeptics and apistics have been trying for centuries to do the same. The boulder they are rolling is one that has been laid haphazardly aside in front of the open mouth of the tomb, and they are desperate to push it back. They mount arguments and complaints that serve to roll that boulder back into place, sealing the tomb up. Yet as soon as they feel like they've gotten close to creating an airtight seal, the boulder rolls aside again. This is their lot for creating smoke and mirrors, for denying clear latent knowledge they have but ignore, for intentionally ignoring their hardwiring—gods condemn tricksters to this sort of thing.

Other Religions Reprised

THE NATURAL FOLLOW-UP question would be, "But aren't other religious faiths embarrassing?" It's a good question that I'd like to press. The initial story of Islam, for instance, profited the Prophet Muhammad greatly, in that it gave him power, land, followers, and as many women as he wanted.[5] Joseph Smith advanced the same way. L. Ron Hubbard got rich. In fact religions and sects formed in the last two thousand years have served to benefit their founders, often in these very same ways. Jesus, recall, never gained any of these things, and instead faced celibacy, poverty, torture, and death. Are these other religions embarrassing? Perhaps aspects, retrospectively. But at the time, they had the look and feel of grand opportunity.

One of the most compelling elements of the story of Jesus is that he is the God who was not embarrassed. He took on human form, which even the early church knew was humiliating (Philippians 2:1-11). Christians worship a God who took the embarrassing route to side with us in our embarrassments. Unlike others who profiteered in founding other religions, he was broke and broken. He chose to be small.

Hardwiring implicates the story of Jesus as embarrassingly true. We all know the temptation to edit the stories of our foibles. Given the opportunity to clean up history, we usually do. There's nothing about the story of Jesus that a good editor couldn't improve, which makes it more likely that the story comes to us in the way it originally happened. All of the human hardwiring points us toward a divine source for morality, identity, and purpose. The hardwiring serves as the final test for a story that claims to answer those needs.

When the final piece snaps into place, only the disingenuous could claim that the piece is merely a figment of wishful thinking. God fits into the human heart because he created the heart to receive him. J. R. R. Tolkien put it this way: "This story begins and ends in joy. It has pre-eminently the 'inner consistency of reality.' There is no tale ever told that men would rather find was true, and none which so many sceptical men have accepted as true on its own merits. For the Art of it has the supremely convincing tone of Primary Art, that is, of Creation. To reject it leads either to sadness or to wrath."[6]

It is the story for which we were made.

Questions for Discussion

1. WHY DO YOU THINK human beings naturally feel embarrassment at certain things?

2. HOW DOES OUR SENSE for embarrassment change the way we tell stories about ourselves?

3. WHY MIGHT THE STORY of Jesus be embarrassing? How many examples can you cite? Are there any you can think of that aren't named in this chapter?

4. HAVE YOU EVER HEARD any plausible explanations for where the story of Jesus might have come from if it was in fact fabricated? Can you dream one up?

5. ARE THERE PARTS of the story of Jesus that seem to you like they could not have been fabricated?

6. IF YOU SHARED the issue of the embarrassing nature of the story of Jesus with a friend who does not believe in him, how do you think your friend would respond?

7. WHAT IS SO SIGNIFICANT about Jesus choosing a humble life rather than a more kingly one?

8. AFTER CONSIDERING the unlikelihood of the fabrication of the story of Jesus life, how has your faith in God changed?

For Prayer and Meditation

THINK ABOUT THE DETAILS of the life of Jesus. Imagine his story if an editor was trying to make Jesus look better. Dwell on the parts of his story that you find most compelling.

7

GOD TALK

The Chair That Wasn't There

IT IS AROUND a campfire that philosophical speculation best lends itself to the formation of deep interpersonal relationships. Something of the primacy of nature brings out the noble savage in us, and we can vulnerably discuss how our most rattling anxieties might be soothed by our most profound ideas. Plus there are s'mores.

It was around a campfire that an atheist friend and I began hammering out the substance of what could be believed in. We covered rituals, holy texts, charismatic cult leaders, and Christmas. He began to take a position of radical doubt, attempting to undermine my hunches and intuitions that had pointed me in the direction of God. He wouldn't acknowledge the reliability of secondhand testimony, ruling out the story of almost all of human history. He wouldn't grant that morality was objective, or that anything religious couldn't merely be a product of biology. However, he then wouldn't substantiate anything he thought dependable in the realm of biology. He really wanted to be a blank slate, one that was particularly resistant to being written upon.

I was getting annoyed.

So at one point in his sermon when he really crescendoed, he insisted that no one in any certain way could prove that the chair that he was sitting on actually existed.

That was a bad move, given the circle of friends he had brought with him to the wilderness. He leaned forward to poke a stick in the fire, lifting himself just a touch off the lawn chair of questionable existence. At that point, a nearby accomplice used the toe of his shoe to scoot the skeptic's chair backward. Just about an inch, mind you, nothing for which he could have been held liable. When my skeptical friend tried to return to his seat, it didn't cause him to fall on his behind. It was worse. It caused him to have that sudden, dramatic, jerky, adrenaline-charged panic with flailing arms as he tried to regain his balance and stop gravity from having its way with him. He stumbled into his chair and saved himself, but at that point he couldn't save his pride. Fortunately what he didn't have in theology he made up for in good humor. It was a good thing, after all, that his chair was really there.

Now what's interesting about the scenario is that my friend was philosophically in about the same place he was physically. He was trying to pull the rug out from underneath himself, the rug he was in fact standing on. That's because talk about God fundamentally requires the existence of God. There are two things in play by the time we strike up a conversation about a deity, and neither of those things could exist if the deity wasn't actually there. This will be very frustrating to the person who believes there is a good reason to reject the existence of God, but one can hardly complain about a chair being yanked away when one is confident it doesn't exist.

Losing Your Marbles

FOR AN ATHEIST to carry on a meaningful conversation about the rejection of God, certain things are required. The first is that the objects in the world around us that we can see actually correspond to our ideas about them in some way. The picture of the chair I have in my head had better be pretty close to one I'm trying to sit on.

This is where the skeptic starts to get into trouble. In a universe empty of God, everything is reduced to the random and causal collision of particles. Picture a landslide of marbles rolling over one another, bouncing, crashing, rebounding, and tumbling. If physics is the science most likely to produce a unified theory of the sciences, sooner or later everything will be reduced to the building blocks of the physical world. All the stars, all the clouds in the sky, all the trees, all the earthworms beneath our feet, all of it is just made of particles that continue to bounce around.

This would then include the particles that make up the gray matter within one's head. That gray matter is just a series of collisions. Where they are not random, they are predetermined. The gelatinous, colored spheres through which light passes into the brain is just the same. It's all just a marble avalanche.

The problem is that when we have a conversation about God, we are fundamentally relying on another assumption we all carry around, specifically, the assumption that the ideas in our head match up pretty well with the objects outside of our head. But if everything is just particles, there is no reason why our brains should have to accurately report on what the world around us holds. There's no reason to trust the particles that make up our brain at the very moment when they are telling us to trust them.[1] C. S. Lewis put it this way: "If minds are wholly dependent on brains, and brains on biochemistry, and biochemistry (in the long run) on the meaningless flux of the atoms, I cannot understand how the thought of those minds should have any more significance than the sound of the wind in the trees."[2]

An atheist can't be sure the chair is there. Nor can he be sure that you are there to debate about it. These are things we've simply assumed, and we carry around the latent sense that something has to make the world objective and our perceptions of it accurate. That simply can't be the case if it's all just particles. As Schopenhauer put it, "Materialism is the philosophy of the subject who forgets to take account of himself."[3] So the atheist can't in the end trust that the ideas that convince him not to believe in God actually correspond to the supposedly godless world around him.

Say What?

TO CONFOUND THINGS, in almost the same way we can't be sure our ideas correspond to the world around us, there is even less reason to assume that the meaning we think we are conveying with our words actually transfers from our mind to the mind of another. If we can't trust the objective world to be objective, we can hardly expect language to communicate anything objective. My friend sitting by the fire thinks he has a real case to make against the existence of God. He looks at the world around him, gets an idea of what it's like, and then tries to convince me that he's seen it correctly. But again, if it's all just particles, there is no reason to assume the particles in his brain correspond to or are even anything like the particles that make up my brain. Here a couple of images are helpful.

Jacques Derrida was a philosopher who wanted to show that language didn't work. He used a lot of words proving his case.[4] It was almost Zen-like. There was one image that he crafted that was particularly beautiful. Derrida was thinking about the way we come up with big ideas from looking at several examples of a big idea. For instance, "justice" is a big concept. Many people think that you can take the big concept and translate it into what you do when you're in a particular argument with a particular friend on a particular Tuesday afternoon. People seem to feel like we have a generally agreed upon idea of "justice" that you and your friend can appeal to in order to decide how to settle your argument. Derrida, however, would say that the way you translated that big idea into your particular situation involved so much bias that he couldn't believe the big idea really existed at all. The word "justice" sounds as if it means something, but it actually does not. Derrida said that if you look closely at the argument you're having, you'd realize that neither you nor your friend have a clearly agreed upon idea of what justice is.[5] Anyone who looks closely enough at how particular words came from big ideas would realize that language doesn't really work when we think it's working.

In this, Derrida is being a pretty good atheist. He sees there is nothing to ground language in reality. He knows materialism has nudged the chair of objectivity out from under human thought. If it's all just particles, we have no reason to believe that my words describe anything real or communicate anything to you.

What's ironic is how many words it takes for him and those like him to say things like this. The deconstructionist project is to turn everything into nothing and then act like they've accomplished something.

Another pretty image comes from another great skeptic. Michel Foucault said that "Truth is undoubtedly the sort of error that cannot be refuted because it was hardened into an unalterable form in the long baking process of history."[6] Language and meaning can hardly be trusted to communicate anything objective. They are so hammered out of shape by bias and confusion that nothing permanent can be assumed from what they produce. Words are as anchored as the wind. Language is as solid as water. Whatever you think may be going on when you have a conversation, don't trust it enough to try and sit on it. You'll find yourself in an arm-waving, adrenaline-charged panic.

Language requires objectivity. And when we talk, we assume there are objective grounds for thinking, perception, and truth-telling. We've latently picked up a sense that something gives grounds to our interactions with a world we believe to be consistently objective. In other words, common experience dictates to us that we can sit down in a chair by the campfire and have a meaningful conversation about things we believe to be true. The problem is there's a latent assumption that lies beneath that simple behavior. We believe our brains have access to objective truth and objective reality. If we are simply particles bouncing around in an empty universe, we have no reason to believe this assumption has any foundation.

Historically, great thinkers have always known and in fact assumed that if anything out there is really objective, it has to be grounded in the mind of God. A number of thinkers have come right out and said it. One great philosopher, Renee Descartes, levels all belief with doubt and then begins building up belief again by starting with the idea that God is the basis for objective truth, or things that are true for everyone.[7] Another philosopher, George Berkeley, said we can only trust things continue to exist when we are not looking at them because God can see them.

This idea coheres poetically with the biblical narrative. God spoke creation into being with a word, and thus everything is held together by the word of God. Dust is a scattering of syllables. Life is order spied in a primordial alphabet soup. DNA is a secret code on biological tablets. God then revealed his will pragmatically through the written law, presented to Moses with a stone foundation of two tablets, the only paper appropriate for such a weighty gift. He is a God of words. Then he stepped into history as the living Word of God, the *logos*, as John called him (John 1:1). Jesus is what happened when God spoke. The annunciation was just God clearing his throat. And then the Word of God had to learn to say "mama." He would go on to say that those who hear his words have a foundation for their lives (Luke 6:46-49). The God of words gives grounding to the world, and it only makes sense that without him our words are vapor.

Trust

IN ORDER TO TALK about God, we must make the assumption that language communicates objective meaning. Another assumption we must make is that conversation is bound by a general commitment to truth-telling. This is a reprise of the point that humanity has a drive to pass on objective morality to the next generation. The best test of the moral case for God's existence comes from the issue of lying. In order to have any conversation at all, we have to be able to assume at some level that the other person shares a mutual commitment to some sort of objective truth.

Gathered around the campfire, arguing ethics, taking an amateur's stab at astronomy, asking about family, telling jokes, and whatever else overflows the heart all require a general agreement to commit to truth-telling. Language has very little purpose if the general assumption cannot be that one is trying to say what one means.

The problem is then a live one. My campfire friend, if he's honest, believes that language is largely a game that allows people to express their will. Language is not a mutual search for the truth. Words are, at best, an attempt to take power by forcing categories onto someone else's ideas. If I make you agree to my definition of justice, then I am more likely to get the kind of justice I want. In the atheist's materialistic perspective, I really don't need to commit to trying to find an objective truth, only the truths that work best for me. I need not pursue things like humility, integrity, honesty, or equality.

So as my friend sits across the fire from me, three things are happening:

- One, he can't trust that the particles bouncing around in his head are actually telling him anything accurate about the real world. When he says that no God exists in the world, I hardly need to care what his particles have come up with. There's no way he can prove his brain particles tell him anything about the real world. "It is an act of faith to assert that our thoughts have any relation to reality at all."[8]
- Two, there's no reason why he himself should believe that his words are effective vehicles for meaning, transferring real ideas from his mind to mine.
- Three, I have no reason to trust that he's committed to an objective truth that he is morally bound to pursue. He could have any number of reasons for the things he's saying, but a moral commitment to truth isn't one of them.

This might seem to be a long way to go to simply get out of an argument that I don't really want to have around the campfire. However, the truth of the matter is that we all have a latent sense that objective truth exists and that we are morally bound to pursue it. We assume it grounds our perceptions in the real world and it grounds meaning in our language. Without it, my friend couldn't really argue that God doesn't exist. The very argument that God doesn't exist depends on a kind of objectivity and truth that only exist in a world with God.

For us to conceive of a natural world made only of particles, we have to trust that we are getting an accurate, objective perception of the world around us. But that is something particles alone can't give us. We have no reason to believe that particles are telling us the truth about particles. Yet we trust our perceptions. That very trust must come from somewhere outside of nature, somewhere above nature. Nature points toward the supernatural.

So in a very real way, an argument that God doesn't exist proves there is a God. At least it proves the person making the argument depends on a world with principles, which could only be reliable if God were really there. So this is the ironic conclusion to this book: whether you've gotten this far believing in God or not, you've proven that you believe the world looks like there must be a God holding it all together.

Questions for Discussion

1. WHAT ARE SOME reasons why people don't understand each other when they talk about big ideas?

2. WHEN DO YOU have trouble putting your ideas into words?

3. HOW DOES GOD give grounding to objective truth? In other words, how does the existence of God guarantee that some things are true for everyone?

4. IF GOD ISN'T THERE, is there anything you can assume is true for everyone?

5. IF EVERYONE BELIEVED, as the atheist must claim, that there is no truth that is objective, what would the world look like?

6. WHY DO WE NEED for certain things to be true for everyone in order to communicate with one another?

7. AT THIS POINT, do you believe that everyone actually knows that God exists or not?

8. WHAT MOST CONVINCES you there must be a God?

9. WHAT MAKES YOU THINK the atheist must be missing something?

For Prayer and Meditation

THINK ABOUT HOW belief in God can give you a sense of confidence and security. Reflect on the things that are assured because God is there.

8
FASTING AND FEASTING

Now Where Are My Keys?

DO YOU REMEMBER the guy in chapter 1 who had lost his keys and couldn't remember where in his brain he had stored the image of the place he left them? We've left him searching a long time. Perhaps it's time to give him some tools that he might use in his search. For those who now have a haunting sense that they are on to something they've been missing, there are three exercises to assist those who want to better see what lies behind our most profound assumptions. These exercises clear our minds enough for us to remember where we left the keys. The clarity that comes from these three exercises should awaken us to the latent knowledge we've unconsciously acquired, giving us a less haunted sense and a more present and aware one. There's a history of spiritual disciplines we can draw on that have allowed people to clear their heads and draw near to the God who is not far from any one of us. This is where *Hardwired* solidly departs from traditional apologetics, the frontal assault on the frontal lobe. This is where we admit the soul is more complex than a blank slate, and it requires more than a heavy dose of facts to come to a knowledge of the truth. If the brain is indeed a searching antennae, we ought to treat it like a living being to be directed toward that which it seems to be looking for. What the curious seeker needs is not more facts to study, but less clutter to distract from the things she already knows.

Remember the Sabbath?

AMERICANS HAVE AN underdeveloped sense of Sabbath and an overdeveloped sense of weekend. We have replaced restoration with relaxation. The consequence is a people who are better versed in football statistics than Scripture. Unless we worship sports or yard work or family, we might better restore the wall that stands between the concept of weekend and the concept of Sabbath.

If we don't set aside time to hear the haunting God within, God can hardly get to any of his most important work. Imagine a doctor who enters a waiting room to meet a patient and finds only a note that the patient has left behind describing his illness. Diagnosis is unlikely and prescriptions are impossible. We need to show up to diagnosis and healing.

God's first object lesson for humanity was this discipline: on the seventh day he rested (Genesis 2:1-3). Exactly how much rest does an omnipotent being need? This was the way the Creator modeled for humanity what was expected of them. They were to recalibrate and remember.

The Sabbath is a day of resetting the hardwiring. We return to the groundwork that lies beneath our most important assumptions to remind ourselves that our hopes are not blind and our beliefs are not arbitrary. Heschel compares this to a return to Eden.[1] We spend one day going back to the creation the way it was supposed to be. It reminds us of that for which we were working.

Imagine the seven days of the week in a heated debate.[2]

"You're lazy," the weekday workdays say to the Sabbath. "We produce everything around here."

"But I am the one for which you produce," the Sabbath might say in return.

Jesus said that the Sabbath is made for humankind and not humankind for the Sabbath (Mark 2:27). This was in contrast to the legalism that was trying to make the rules of dinner table etiquette more important than the diners. The food is made for the patron, not vice versa. The corollary that cannot be ignored is that the week was made for the Sabbath, not the Sabbath for the week. Humanity in a state of uninterrupted attention to God is primary to humanity working the ground of God's creation.

The Sabbath is the way we stop assuming. We stop functioning on latent knowledge and start really knowing. We remind ourselves what the completed puzzle is supposed to look like. So when we return to a gray and dreary world in which moral clarity is obscured by broken humanity, we can remember that the hardwiring is still pointing us in the right direction: toward the next Sabbath and our next communion with God.

One Foot In

I REMEMBER STANDING in the Chicago airport in
January. I had gone for a friend's wedding, and standing in
Chicago in January made me question how good a friend
he had been. I was dressed in more layers than an onion,
of shirts and jackets and long underwear and sweaters and
socks on top of socks.

I was returning to Hawaii, where I lived at the time.
The Chicago winter was my friend's revenge for an envi-
ous calling to ministry in a tropical paradise. I couldn't wait
to get home. Apparently, I wasn't alone in my anticipation.
A married couple well into middle age was headed in the
same direction, as everyone could tell from the fact that they
were dressed head to toe in matching aloha wear. They both
had straw hats. They both had red shirts emblazoned with
surfboards. They had red shorts. It made me cold to look at
them.

I couldn't resist sidling up alongside them and asking
them, "So where are you guys headed?"

They answered excitedly, "We're going to Hawaii!"

They were so enthusiastic about escaping the Chicago
cold to make it to the Hawaiian sun that they were already
dressed for the place they were going. They were so ready
for it that they no longer even looked like they belonged at
the place where they were.

It made me wonder why few who call themselves
Christian and seem to be headed toward eternity actually
dress for their anticipated future. The Sabbath is a basic

way to plan for the eternal vacation in paradise. Without the Sabbath, our weekly recognition of the Eden from which we came and the New Earth to which we will return falls by the wayside. The Sabbath helps us notice the hardwiring that has been pointing us in the right direction all along.

A Primer in Fasting

AFTER TIME TO RESTORE and rest, fasting is the second spiritual discipline that helps us see the hardwiring again. If the Sabbath is Eden, fasting is the act of refusing the fruit that Eve picked. It is abstaining from that which does not nourish so as to return to the presence of God.

What fasting does is causally tied to the way the hardwiring works. It's actually very logical.

Kindergarteners do an experiment with nature. They take a moist bean and place it in a plastic cup filled with fresh, musty soil. The cup is intentionally clear, and the bean is lodged alongside the edge of the cup. As it sprouts, the children can watch the roots grow down and the leaves grow up, until the top explodes like a cresting dolphin and the bottom spindles through the earth with spider-like tentacles. Now a clever teacher might teach the children another lesson. Before the shoots break the top of the earth, the cup can be laid on its side. When it is, the plant makes an almost ninety degree turn and begins growing sideways within the cup. At this rate, it will never escape the ground in which it is buried. The plant is not reaching toward the air; it's reaching toward the sun.

The human soul is hardwired for the sun. We grow toward the light that will most fully nourish us. Given a steady intake of stimuli, we might easily turn to relationships, affirmation, accomplishment, caffeine, entertainment, ecstasy, distraction, and daydreaming. We'll gladly grab at whatever light is closest and brightest. It's how we're wired.

Fasting is the act of turning out all other distracting lights. It's the act of letting your soul grow in the direction it was meant to.

Imagine the night sky seen from the perspective of an urban street versus the same overhead canopy when viewed from an empty desert road on a summer night. Overhead are a pantheon of angelic shapes covered with twinkling eyes in front and in back. The ancients found among them shapes of things like a lion or an ox or a man or an eagle. They are there all the time, watching over the world, but lesser lights usually blind us from them. It's only when the smaller lights go out that we can see the electric pathways of the heavens.

Fasting helps us see what is there all along, though we are usually blind to the "greater lights." The heavens proclaim God's glory, so much so that the constellations at the four corners of the sky cannot help but call out, "Holy, holy, holy."

Usually we miss it.

This again calls to mind the traditional apologists who have so desperately sought to prove the existence of God by hammering away at the mind. The heart has always been wired for God, and the starry world above and the moral world within are enough to show everyone that he is there.[3] Traditional apologists think they can satisfy the mind without engaging the soul. This makes apologetics itself a lesser light, preventing us from seeing how the heart and the hardwiring are made.

For any of us who have a sense that there's something buried in our hardwiring, something upon which we've been depending without taking much notice of it, we might come to realize how clear the heavenly display is by turning out all the other lights.

Feasting

FASTING, HOWEVER, IS NOT an end in itself. It's the act of blocking out the unnecessary to make room for the unavoidable. That which is essential to life then takes the place of the things we just as well rid ourselves of. In that way, fasting leads to feasting.

This third spiritual discipline that awakens us to our foundational assumptions is meditation. Meditation is to prayer what Mary was to Martha (Luke 10:38-42). Martha ran around trying to do things for Jesus while Mary simply listened to him. Prayer tends to be full of requests; meditation simply waits. If prayer is the active initiation of the worshiper, meditation is the act of listening quietly for

God's response to our prayers, and meditation aids us, once we have cleared out the distraction, to choose the better lights.

Meditation envisions the Eden toward which we are trying to return every Sabbath. We fast to be free, and then we dwell on a vision of what real freedom looks like. Meditation is gorging on the vision of a life of love, joy, and peace. It's lying in soft grass and finding shapes in the clouds. It's reflecting on what life would be like if all the little inclinations of the existence of God were as loud as cymbals and as bright as the sun.

Meditation does not involve contorting one's self into the lotus position while inhaling incense. It's simply the concerted effort of listening to God, then gathering a vision of the kind of life that God wants for you, and finally setting out to accomplish it. Meditation is like the architect imagining the final cathedral before drawing up the blueprints. It's projecting a vision of what is to come so that the architect's drawing—every line of it—is headed in the right direction, filling in the big picture.

It's like the little boy who sat at his kitchen table drawing a picture. His father looked over his shoulder and asked, "What are you drawing, son?"

"I'm drawing a picture of God," the boy said.

"No one can draw a picture of God, silly," his dad corrected. "No one has ever seen God. No one knows what God looks like."

"Well," responded the boy, "they'll know when I finish my picture, won't they?"

Meditation is that act of imagining what God would look like, what God's kingdom would look like, what tomorrow lived in the footsteps of Jesus would look like. And then the meditator goes and lives it.

A New Apology

ARGUMENTS FOR THE EXISTENCE of God usually have ended at the scales or the calculator, tabulating to see whose rationale carried the most weight or scored the most points. But the search for God should begin in poetry and end in song. The fact that apologists have gone at this ineffectively is just one more sign that we've lost sight of the hardwiring. No one looking at the foundational assumptions and needs of the human heart would ever have walked away from a debate saying, "Wow, that missing piece is a good debate."

What convicts us of the existence of God is not hard facts or arguments but the soft, subjective facts of an experience that resonates with human longing and confirms our deep suspicions. When we get to the place we were meant to be, there is nothing left to calculate and no desire to weigh the results. No one has to convince you that you're home. When you've made space to pay attention to the hardwiring and cut out the distractions, a bigger picture unfolds, and the last puzzle piece snaps into place.

Questions for Discussion

1. DO YOU THINK anyone can be argued into believing in God? What role do you think argumentation and belief play in someone coming to believe in God?

2. WHY MIGHT PEOPLE have trouble keeping the Sabbath?

3. HOW COULD YOU benefit from a Sabbath day?

4. IN TERMS OF FASTING, what in your life distracts you from things that are meaningful?

5. WHAT MIGHT BE the benefits of fasting?

6. DO YOU THINK you can commit to taking a day to focus on God, putting aside the things that might distract you from him and dwelling on the world that he created? What might help you keep this commitment?

7. HOW MIGHT YOUR LIFE change if you had a weekly day of remembering what your life is for?

For Prayer and Meditation

REMEMBER THE SABBATH day and keep it holy. On that day, don't do any work. Instead, abstain from distractions and focus on the God who made you for him.

9
THE LAST PIECE

A MAN ONCE TOLD ME, "I believe in God, but I'm not ready for him yet." I doubt very much the belief that has no time for itself. I suspect the guy hadn't yet realized where the gaps in the puzzle of his existence were and what might best go into them.

If God is there, everything has changed. And likewise if God is not there, everything has changed. Everything depends on a decision we make about that key question. It will either resolve the puzzle or it won't. And anyone who has had a go at a jigsaw puzzle knows sometimes the best method is to grab the next available piece and see if it fits in. What this book has tried to do is point out that all of the colors and contours of the puzzle seem to be begging for a theological completion.

This is not a God-of-the-gaps idea, at least no more than a materialist answer is a particles-of-the-gaps idea. On the subject of gaps, a strange alternative is offered by philosopher Colin McGinn. He wrestles with the reality that the consciousness of the human mind is something that arises out of certain combinations of cells and not others.[1] Brains are conscious, but fingers aren't, despite the fact that they're made out of the same kind of particles. There is no reason, he points out, why consciousness should arise from meat at all. There is all sorts of meat in the world, and only the brain produces consciousness. "How did evolution convert the water of biological tissue into the wine of consciousness?"[2]

he asks. His conclusion is that we don't know and can't know. The answer to that question is something that lies beyond the exploratory powers of consciousness. The brain just can't see into the mechanism that makes consciousness arise from the brain. And that's that. You wonder why theologians are accused of stopgap measures when materialists have nothing better to offer. At the end of the day, we have picked up a latent awareness that we depend on certain assumptions. The foundations that lie behind those assumptions are most definitely filling gaps, but the theistic foundation makes more sense than the materialist's final "Dunno."

So when the materialist's piece doesn't bring the puzzle to resolve, it's only logical that the person assembling the puzzle would try the next piece. Let's see. What shape is it? It creates a purpose for life, as though life came from somewhere and is going somewhere. It gives life a sense of deep rights and wrongs. It makes people want truth and depend on truth. In fact it leaves us naked when we realize we're embarrassingly less than perfect.

Peace is the act of putting the final puzzle piece where it belongs. You can only tell it belongs there when you try it.

Questions for Discussion

1. DO YOU BELIEVE in God? Why or why not?

2. WHAT IS THE MOST compelling reason for believing in God that you've discovered in *Hardwired*?

3. WHAT IS THE BEST reason you've ever heard for not believing in God?

4. ARE THERE WAYS you now think that you've been depending on God without acknowledging him?

5. ARE THERE SIGNS of God's existence you see in the world or in your life that have not been covered in *Hardwired*?

6. HOW DO YOU THINK someone should live if they are convinced they were created by a loving God?

7. IN ROMANS 1:20, why do you think Paul uses the language of being "without excuse" for not believing in God?

8. IF YOU TALK to other people about God's place in your life and in theirs, what response do you anticipate?

9. WHAT QUESTION about God is most pressing on your heart today, and where might you go to further explore that question?

10. IS THERE SOMEONE ELSE with whom you might discuss *Hardwired*?

For Prayer and Meditation

IF THERE ARE ANY OBJECTIONS you still have to believing in God, think about who you might talk to or what you might read to go on sorting them out. If not, picture tomorrow as the first day in which you wake up with an absolutely confident faith. What will tomorrow look like?

ACKNOWLEDGMENTS

I DEEPLY APPRECIATE the many people who have helped me arrive at the day on which I am required to write a page of acknowledgements. Thanks go to: Lil Copan and Abingdon Press for creating such a streamlined, encouraging, and fun process; the people of Glenkirk Church, who have made me happy to be a pastor; Betty Liu, for starting my writing career; Dan Chun, who coached me; Earl Palmer, who taught me; my parents and Susan, who shaped me; and Yolanda, Sonoma, and Koen, who helped me see things I would have missed. And to Phil Yancey, who told me it only takes one bestseller.

BIBLIOGRAPHY

Aquinas, Thomas. *Summa Theologica*. New York: Benziger, 1948.

Aristotle. *Metaphysics*. Translated by W. D. Ross. New York: Penguin Books, 2009.

———. *On the Heavens*. Translated by W. K. C. Guthrie. Boston: Harvard University Press, 1939.

Augustine. *Confessions*. New York: Oxford University Press, 2009.

Begley, Sharon and Anne Underwood. "Religion and the Brain," *Newsweek*, May 7, 2001.

Bentham, Jeremy. *The Works of Jeremy Bentham*. Edited by John Bowring. Edinburgh: William Tate, 1843.

Biello, David. "Searching for God in the Brain." *Scientific American Mind*, Oct/Nov 2007.

Camus, Albert. "The Myth of Sisyphus." In *The Myth of Sisyphus and Other Essays*. New York: Vintage Books, 1991.

———. *The Plague*. Translated by Robin Buss. Toronto: Penguin, 2004.

Chesterton, G. K. *Orthodoxy*. New York: Simon and Brown, 2012.

Cicero, Marcus Tullius. *Cicero's Tusculan Disputations; Also, Treatises On The Nature Of The Gods, And On The Commonwealth*. Qontro Classic Books, 2010.

Craig, William Lane. *The Kalam Cosmological Argument*. Eugene, OR: Wipf and Stock, 2000.

————. *Reasonable Faith: Christian Truth and Apologetics*. 3rd ed. Wheaton, IL: Crossway Books, 2008.

De Botton, Alain. *The Architecture of Happiness*. New York: Vintage Books, 2006.

Descartes, Renee. *Meditations on First Philosophy*. New York: Simon and Brown, 2011.

————. *Religion for Atheists: A Non-believer's Guide to the Uses of Religion*. New York: Vintage Books, 2013.

Dulles, Avery Cardinal. *A History of Apologetics*. San Francisco: Ignatius Press, 2005.

Foucault, Michel. "Nietzsche, Genealogy, History." In *The Foucault Reader*. Edited by Paul Rabinow. New York: Pantheon, 1984. Freud, Sigmund. *The Future of an Illusion*. Seattle, WA: CreateSpace Independent Publishing Platform, 2010.

Gould, Stephen Jay. "Sociobiology and the Theory of Natural Selection." In *Sociobiology: Beyond Nature/Nurture?* Edited by G. W. Barlow and J. Silverberg. Boulder, CO: Westview Press, 1980.

Heath, Chip and Dan Heath. *Switch: How to Change the World When Change Is Hard*. New York: Crown Business, 2010.

Heraclitus. *Fragments*. New York: Penguin Classics, 2001.

Herodotus. *The Histories*. New York: Penguin Classics, 2003.

Heschel, Abraham Joshua. *The Sabbath*. New York: Farrar Straus Giroux, 2005.

Hitchens, Christopher. "Does God Exist?" Debate at Biola University, La Mirada, CA, April 4, 2009.

Huxley, Thomas. "Agnosticism: A Rejoinder." In *Collected Essays of Thomas Huxley: Science and Christian Tradition*, vol. 5. Whitefish, MT: Kessinger, 2005.

James, William. *The Varieties of Religious Experience: A Study in Human Nature*. New York: Oxford University Press, 2012.

Jefferson, Thomas. *The Jefferson Bible: The Life and Morals of Jesus of Nazareth*. Radford, VA: Wilder, 2007.

Kahneman, Daniel, et al. "Would You Be Happier If You Were Richer? A Focusing Illusion." May 2006, http://www.morgen kommichspaeterrein.de/ressources/download/125krueger.

Kant, Immanuel. *Critique of Practical Reason*. New York: Classic Books International, 2010.

———. *Critique of Pure Reason*. Translated by J. M. D. Meiklejohn. Buffalo: Prometheus Books, 1990.

Keller, Timothy. *The Reason for God*. New York: Riverhead Trade, 2009.

Kluger, Jeffrey. "The Biology of Belief." *Time,* February 12, 2009.

Loconte, Joseph. *The Searchers: A Quest for Faith in the Valley of Doubt*. Nashville: Thomas Nelson, 2012.

Lewis, C. S. "Is Theology Poetry?" In *The Weight of Glory*. New York: HarperCollins, 1980.

———. *Mere Christianity*. New York: Touchstone, 1980.

———. *Surprised by Joy: The Shape of My Early Life*. Orlando: Harcourt, Brace, 1955.

Locke, John. *An Essay Concerning Human Understanding*. Edited by J. W. Yolton. London: Everyman, 1994.

Mackey, Louis H. and John Searle. "An Exchange on Deconstruction." In *The New York Review of Books,* February 2, 1984.Marcus Aurelius. *Meditations*. Hollywood, FL: Simon and Brown, 2012.

McGinn, Colin. *The Mysterious Flame: Conscious Minds in a Material World*. New York: Basic Books, 1999.

Medina, John. *Brain Rules: 12 Principles for Surviving and Thriving at Work, Home, and School*. Seattle, WA: Pear Press, 2009.

Meier, John P. *A Marginal Jew: Rethinking the Historical Jesus,* vol 1. Anchor Bible Reference Library. New York: Doubleday, 1991.

Miller, Calvin. *The Singer: A Classic Retelling of Cosmic Conflict*. Downers Grove, IL: InterVarsity Press, 2001.

Moore, G. E. *Principia Ethica*. Cambridge: Cambridge University Press, 2000.

National Geographic. "The Genographic Project." https://genographic.nationalgeographic.com/genographic/participate.html

Niebuhr, Rienhold. *Faith and History*. New York: Scribner, 1949.

Nowak, Martin A., Corina E. Tarnita, and Edward O. Wilson. "The Evolution of Eusociality." *Nature* 466, August 26, 2010.

Nozick, Robert. *Invariances: The Structure of the Objective World*. Cambridge, MA: Belknap Press of Harvard University Press, 2003.

Ortberg, John. *The Me I Want to Be*. Grand Rapids: Zondervan, 2010.

Otto, Rudolph. *The Idea of the Holy*. New York: Oxford University Press, 1958.

Ovid. *Metamorphoses*. Translated by David Raeburn. New York: Penguin Classics, 2004.

Pascal, Blaise. *Pensees*. Translated by A. J. Krailsheimer. New York: Penguin Books, 1980.

Philo. *The Works of Philo: Complete and Unabridged*. Peabody, MA: Hendrickson, 1993.

Piaget, Jean. *The Language and Thought of the Child*. New York: Routledge Classics, 1959.

Pinker, Steven. *The Blank Slate: The Modern Denial of Human Nature*. New York: Viking, 2002.

Plato. *The Collected Dialogues*. Edited by Edith Hamilton and Huntington Cairns. Princeton: Princeton University Press, 2005.

Rescher, Nicholas. "Choice Without Preference: A Study of the History and of the Logic of the Problem of 'Buridan's Ass.'" *Kant-Studien* 51 (1960):142–75.

Russell, Bertrand. "Why I Am Not A Christian." In *On God and Religion*. Edited by Al Seckel. Amherst, NY: Prometheus Books, 1986.

Sartre, Jean-Paul. *Existentialism Is a Humanism*. New Haven: Yale University Press, 2007.

Searle, John. *The Mystery of Consciousness*. New York: New York Review of Books, 1997.

Schiller, Friedrich Von. *Letters Upon the Aesthetic Education of Man*. Mineola, NY: Dover Press, 2004.

Schopenhauer, Arthur. *The World as Will and Representation*, vol. 2. Translated by E. F. J. Payne. Indian Hills, CO: Courier Dover, 1966.

Strobel, Lee. *The Case for Christ: A Journalist's Personal Investigation of the Evidence for Jesus*. Grand Rapids: Zondervan, 1998.

Taylor, Charles. *A Secular Age*. Cambridge, MA: Belknap Press of Harvard University Press, 2007.

Tolkien, J. R. R. "On Fairy Stories." In *Essays Presented to Charles Williams*. Edited by C. S. Lewis. Grand Rapids: Eerdmans, 1966.

Willard, Dallas. Lecture at Fuller Theological Seminary course at Mater Dolorosa Retreat Center, July 2012.

Wilson, Edward O. "The Biological Basis of Morality." In *The Atlantic Online*. April 1998. http://www.theatlantic.com/past/docs/issues/98apr/biomoral.htm

NOTES

Introduction

1. Augustine, *Confessions* (New York: Oxford University Press, 2009), III.xii.21.

1. What You Didn't Know You Knew

1. I'm focusing on the work of Protestant apologists in the United States in the latter half of the twentieth century, particularly those within the circles of Wolfhart Pannenberg (Avery Cardinal Dulles, *A History of Apologetics* [San Francisco: Ignatius Press, 2005], 351–58).

2. "'Nones' on the Rise: One-in-Five Adults Have No Religious Affiliation," *The Pew Forum on Religion and Public Life,* October 9, 2012.

3. PBS *Firing Line* Debate, December 19, 1997.

4. Cf. William Lane Craig, *Reasonable Faith: Christian Truth and Apologetics*, 3rd ed. (Wheaton: Crossway Books, 2008), 5–12. Craig argues for the place of apologetics as a preventative measure against cultural secularism on the one side and fundamentalism on the other. However, he equivocates between the value of Christian apologetics specifically and intellectual integrity generally. He doesn't demonstrate that Christian apologetics actually address the means by which people come to faith. He goes on to aptly compare apologetics with the work of a

missionary reaching a minority of the population. In all fairness to Craig, he is an advocate of a version of natural theology and appends his work with the caveat that personal experience of God without scholarly verification is nonetheless valid.

5. Steven Pinker, *The Blank Slate: The Modern Denial of Human Nature* (New York: Viking, 2002), esp. 121–36.

6. Later I will deal with the objection that human brokenness is such that intuition is now hopelessly marred.

7. Reinhold Niebuhr said that the goal of apologetics "consists in correlating the truth, apprehended by faith and repentance, to truths about life and history, gained generally in experience." (Reinhold Niebuhr, *Faith and History* [New York: Scribner, 1949], 164–65). Life leaves behind a series of blanks that faith fills in.

8. Edward O. Wilson observed, "Rarely do we see an argument that opens with the simple statement *This is my starting point, and it could be wrong.*" (Edward O. Wilson, "The Biological Basis of Morality," *The Atlantic Online,* April 1998, http://www.theatlantic.com/past/docs/issues/98apr/biomoral.htm)

9. C. S. Lewis, *Mere Christianity* (New York: Touchstone, 1980), 17.

10. An example of this is Plato's *Meno,* in which Socrates dismantles someone else's apparently meaningless definition of virtue.

11. This perhaps explains the structure of Psalm 19. It goes from an acknowledgment of signs of God's existence in creation (vv. 1-6) to the revelation of God is his Law (vv. 7-11) to confession (vv. 11-14). Existentially, the sudden awareness of the presence of God carries with it the implication that we should have known, that we missed it, and that our finitude necessitates our humility.

2. The Hardwiring

1. Charles Taylor, *A Secular Age* (Cambridge, MA: Belknap Press of Harvard University Press, 2007), 29–41. Taylor's expansive genealogy of secularism is awe-inspiring.

2. John Locke, *An Essay Concerning Human Understanding,* ed. J. W. Yolton (London: Everyman, 1994), 17.

3. Steven Pinker, *The Blank Slate: The Modern Denial of Human Nature* (New York: Viking), 2002, esp. pp. 121–36.

4. This was at the heart of the Kantian revolution, spawned by a very similar issue. Hume's antagonistic doubt awakened Kant to the reality that the human mind could not sustain the position of unaffected skepticism. The mind was far too active for that. Similarly, modern neuroscience has begun to expose the complexities of the active brain. Cf. John Medina, *Brain Rules: 12 Principles for Surviving and Thriving at Work, Home, and School* (Seattle: Pear Press, 2009).

5. Daniel Kahneman et al., "Would You Be Happier If You Were Richer? A Focusing Illusion," Princeton University Center for Economic Policy Studies Working Paper No. 125, May 2006, http://www.morgenkommichspaeterrein.de/ressources/download/125krueger.

6. I discovered after writing this that John Ortberg has used a similar metaphor for different purposes in *The Me I Want to Be* (Grand Rapids: Zondervan, 2010), 36–37.

7. John Searle, *The Mystery of Consciousness* (New York: New York Review of Books, 1997), 5.

8. Jean Piaget, *The Language and Thought of the Child* (New York: Routledge Classics, 1959), 3639.

9. "It is certain, and evident to our sense, that in the world some things are in motion. Now whatever is moved is moved by another, for nothing can be moved except it is in potentiality to that towards which it is moved; whereas a thing moves inasmuch as it is in act. For motion is

nothing else than the reduction of something from potentiality to actuality. But nothing can be moved from a state of potentiality to actuality, except by something in a state of actuality . . . it is therefore impossible that in the same respect and in the same way a thing should be both mover and moved i.e., that it should move itself. Therefore, whatever is moved must be moved by another. If that by which it is moved must itself be moved, then this also needs to be moved by another, and that by another again. But this cannot go on to infinity, because then there would be no first mover, and consequently, no other mover, seeing as subsequent movers move only inasmuch as they are moved by the first mover; as the staff moves only because it is moved by the hand. Therefore it is necessary to arrive at the first mover, moved by no other; and this everyone understands to be God." (Thomas Aquinas, *Summa Theologica,* I, 2, iii).

10. The charge can be leveled that God would then be an odd exception to the rule that everything in motion must have been moved by something else. Some have cleverly evaded that charge by suggesting that an unmoved God moves everything else by drawing the world to himself while he sits still. I intend to avoid the charge by not reading Aquinas. I just wanted you to know that I'm not the first person who noticed all of this motion going on and wondered what it meant.

11. T. H. Huxley, "Agnosticism: A Rejoinder," in *Collected Essays of Thomas Huxley: Science and Christian Tradition,* vol. 5. (Whitefish, MT: Kessinger, 2005).

12. Bertrand Russell, "What Is an Agnostic?" in *Look* (November 3, 1953), in Bertrand Russell, *On God And Religion,* ed. Al Seckel (Amherst, NY: Prometheus Books, 1986), 73–82.

13. Augustine, *Confessions* (New York: Oxford University Press, 2009), 3.

14. Aristotle, *On the Heavens,* trans. W. K. C. Guthrie (Boston: Harvard University Press, 1939), 2.13.3.

15. Analogy from William Lane Craig, http://www.reasonablefaith. org/molinism. Cf. Nicholas Rescher, "Choice Without Preference: A Study of the History and of the Logic of the Problem of 'Buridan's Ass,'" *Kant-Studien* 51, no. 1–4 (1960):142–75.

16. Cf. Craig, *Reasonable Faith: Christian Truth and Apologetics,* 3rd ed., (Wheaton, IL: Crossway Books, 2008), 58–72.

17. Jean-Paul Sartre, *Existentialism Is a Humanism* (New Haven: Yale University Press, 2007).

18. Only the later insertion of vowels distinguishes the two words.

19. Cf. Timothy Keller, *The Reason for God* (New York: Riverhead Trade, 2009), 127–28. Keller points out that there is no strongly rational proof for "strong rationalism."

3. Belief on the Brain

1. Christopher Hitchens admitted that while claiming to be one of the "New Atheists," he really had nothing new to add to atheism. ("Does God Exist?" debate at Biola University, La Mirada, CA, April 4, 2009).

2. Loconte writes, "Every civilization, without fail, develops an elaborate system of religious beliefs that help to hold human societies together" (Joseph Loconte, *The Searchers: A Quest for Faith in the Valley of Doubt* [Nashville: Thomas Nelson, 2012], 4).

3. C. S. Lewis, *Surprised by Joy: The Shape of My Early Life* (Orlando: Harcourt Brace, 1955), 226.

4. William James, *The Varieties of Religious Experience: A Study in Human Nature* (New York: Oxford University Press, 2012), lectures 16 and 17.

5. Ibid., lecture 19. While it probably doesn't need to be pursued here, Freidrich Schiller makes a sort of mystical/materialistic equivalent of art. In almost religious terms he describes how "Humanity has lost its dignity, but Art has rescued it and preserved it." (*Letters Upon*

the Aesthetic Education of Man [Mineola, NY: Dover Press, 2004], 52.) Schiller perceives a transcended form or ideal in art that lifts him from the material world. Beauty might be said to be just another signpost of God.

6. This term is credited to Aldous Huxley, grandson of Thomas Huxley, the creator of "agnostic."

7. Sharon Begley with Anne Underwood, "Religion and the Brain," *Newsweek*, May 7, 2001, 50.

8. A good summary of the research is in David Biello's "Searching for God in the Brain," *Scientific American Mind,* Oct/Nov 2007, 39–45.

9. Edward O. Wilson, "The Biological Basis of Morality," *The Atlantic Online,* April 1998, http://www.theatlantic.com/past/docs/issues/98apr/biomoral.htm. Wilson, curiously, is a provisional deist, meaning he suspects there is something out there beyond the material world, but chooses to find his reasons for everything within matter, thus having and eating his theological cake.

10. Jeffrey Kluger, "The Biology of Belief," *Time,* February 12, 2009.

11. I'm not giving time for the objection one might hear, that "Wait! You haven't proven that the religious desire is not a misplaced desire for something else! What if we're just looking for a father figure?" That objection sounds to me like someone saying, "Wait! You haven't proven that your hunger is actually a desire for food and not something else!" Food is, almost by definition, that which satisfies hunger, and God is, almost by definition, that which satisfies the religious instinct.

12. Cicero, *De Natura Deorum* II, 28. "Persons who spent whole days in prayer and sacrifice to ensure that their children should out-live them were termed 'superstitious' (from *supersies,* a survivor), and the word later acquired a wider application. Those on the other hand who carefully reviewed and so to speak retraced all the lore of ritual were called 'religious' from *relegere* (to retrace or re-read). . . . Hence 'super-

stitious' and 'religious' came to be terms of censure and approval respectively. I think that I have said enough to prove the existence of the gods and their nature."

13. See James' opening chapters on exploring the religious instinct.

14. Alain De Botton, *The Architecture of Happiness* (New York: Vintage Books, 2006), 112.

15. De Botton gives himself away in *Religion for Atheists* (New York: Vintage, 2013). In it, he describes how his atheist father demeaned his eight-year-old sister until she cried because she dared to hope for God. De Botton, I think, is still afraid of paternal voices.

4. Absolutely

1. Stephen Jay Gould, "Sociobiology and the Theory of Natural Selection," in *Sociobiology: Beyond Nature/Nurture?* ed. George W. Barlow and James Silverberg (Boulder, CO: Westview, 1980), 257.

2. William Lane Craig, *Reasonable Faith: Christian Truth and Apologetics,* 3rd ed. (Wheaton: Crossway Books, 2008), chap. 2.

3. Cf. Edward O. Wilson, "The Biological Basis of Morality," *The Atlantic Online,* April 1998, http://www.theatlantic.com/past/docs/issues/98apr/biomoral.htm. Wilson, in fact, traces what he believes to be the process by which ethics moved from tribal survival to abstract religious ideals. He admits that principles arrived at thus can ultimately be abandoned over time.

4. For some time there has been a desperate attempt to explain how genes best preserve themselves by supporting a family culture in which they may survive through kin rather than through a given individual. Thus it may be advantageous to the individual to sacrifice itself for the preservation of kin. This, however, is still being debated and is referred to by sociobiologists as "theoretical attempts" to explain good behavior. That terminology is the scientific baptism of a guess. See the criticism of this

theory in "The Evolution of Eusociality," Martin A. Nowak, Corina E. Tarnita, and Edward O. Wilson, *Nature* 466, August 26, 2010: 1057–62.

5. Jeremy Bentham, "Critique of the Doctrine of Inalienable, Natural Rights," *The Works of Jeremy Bentham,* vol. 2, ed. John Bowring (Edinburgh: William Tate, 1843).

6. Bentham, "Of Slavery," *The Works of Jeremy Bentham,* vol. 1.

7. Sigmund Freud, *The Future of an Illusion* (Seattle, WA: CreateSpace Independent Publishing Platform), 2010.

5. Coming and Going

1. https://genographic.nationalgeographic.com/genographic/partici pate.html

2. G. E. Moore tries to argue the opposite in his *Principia Ethica.* I say "argue" in a loose sense, because it actually isn't argued so much as just stated. Moore wants to say that value exists within objects in the same way yellowness exists within yellow objects. "Good" cannot be defined any more than "yellow," because it is simply the collective experience of good instances (G. E. Moore, *Principia Ethica* [Cambridge: Cambridge University Press, 2000], 59).

3. William L. Craig, *The Kalam Cosmological Argument* (Eugene, OR: Wipf and Stock, 2000).

4. Abraham Heschel, *The Sabbath* (New York: Farrar Straus Giroux, 2005), esp. chap. 1.

5. Albert Camus plays with this theme in his works of fiction, wondering what it might mean to be a saint without God. See *The Plague,* trans. Robin Buss (Toronto: Penguin, 2004).

6. Chip Heath and Dan Heath, *Switch: How to Change the World When Change Is Hard* (New York: Crown Business, 2010), 47.

7. Hugh of St. Victor, quoted in Alain De Botton, *The Architecture of Happiness* (New York: Vintage Books, 2006), 149.

8. Albert Camus, "The Myth of Sisyphus," in *The Myth of Sisyphus and Other Essays* (New York: Vintage, 1991), 150.

9. Calvin Miller, *The Singer: A Classic Retelling of Cosmic Conflict* (Downers Grove, IL: InterVarsity, 2001), 40.

10. Aristotle, *Metaphysics,* trans. W. D. Ross (New York: Penguin Books, 2009), 1049b18–19.

6. How Embarrassing

1. "The point of the criterion is that the early Church would hardly have gone out of its way to create material that only embarrassed its creator or weakened its position in arguments with opponents." (John P. Meier, *A Marginal Jew: Rethinking the Historical Jesus,* Anchor Bible Reference Library, vol. 1 [New York: Doubleday, 1991], 168.)

2. Thomas Jefferson, *The Jefferson Bible: The Life and Morals of Jesus of Nazareth* (Radford, VA: Wilder, 2007).

3. Blaise Pascal, *Pensees,* trans. A. J. Krailsheimer (New York: Penguin Books, 1980), (X: 148), 75.

4. Bertrand Russell, "Why I Am Not A Christian," in *Bertrand Russell on God And Religion,* ed. Al Seckel (Amherst, NY: Prometheus Books, 1986), 66.

5. The Qur'an, 33:50.

6. J. R. R. Tolkien, "On Fairy Stories," in *Essays Presented to Charles Williams,* ed. C. S. Lewis (Grand Rapids: Eerdmans, 1966).

7. God Talk

1. The alternative view, generally called "naive realism," simply states that you can know because you know. This is what normal people would call an unfounded assumption.

2. C. S. Lewis, "Is Theology Poetry?" in *The Weight of Glory* (New York: HarperCollins, 1980), 139.

3. Arthur Schopenhauer, *The World as Will and Representation,* vol. 2, trans. E. F. J. Payne (Indian Hills, CO: Courier Dover, 1966), 13.

4. John Searle criticized Derrida by saying, "Anyone who reads deconstructive texts with an open mind is likely to be struck by the same phenomena that initially surprised me: the low level of philosophical argumentation, the deliberate obscurantism of the prose, the wildly exaggerated claims, and the constant striving to give the appearance of profundity by making claims that seem paradoxical, but under analysis often turn out to be silly or trivial." (Louis H. Mackey and John Searle, "An Exchange on Deconstruction," *The New York Review of Books,* vol. 1, February 2, 1984).

5. John D. Caputo, *The Prayers and Tears of Jacques Derrida: Religion Without Religion* (Bloomington: Indiana University Press, 1997), 25, 138, 245.

6. Michel Foucault, "Nietzsche, Genealogy, History," in *The Foucault Reader,* ed. Paul Rabinow (New York: Pantheon, 1984), 79.

7. Renee Descartes, *Meditations on First Philosophy* (New York: Simon and Brown, 2011).

8. G. K. Chesterton, *Orthodoxy* (New York: Simon and Brown, 2012), 30.

8. Fasting and Feasting

1. Abraham Joshua Heschel, *The Sabbath* (New York: Farrar Straus Giroux, 2005),15.

2. Ibid., 39.

3. Immanuel Kant, *Critique of Practical Reason* (New York: Classic Books International, 2010). Kant even had this famous line inscribed on his tombstone: "Two things fill the mind with ever new and increasing

admiration and law, the oftener and more steadily we reflect on them: the starry heavens above and the moral law within."

9. The Last Piece

1. Colin McGinn, *The Mysterious Flame: Conscious Minds in a Material World* (New York: Basic Books, 1999), 1–30.

2. Ibid., 13.

JAMES W. MILLER is senior pastor of the dynamic Glenkirk Church in San Gabriel Valley, California, and has degrees from Fuller Seminary, Princeton Seminary, and UC Berkeley. He is a frequent speaker at conferences, graduations, and camps. He and his wife, Yolanda, live in Glendora, California. Visit www.pastorjamesmiller.com.